SECURE ENOUGH?

SECURE ENOUGH?

20 QUESTIONS
ON **CYBERSECURITY**
FOR **BUSINESS OWNERS**
AND **EXECUTIVES**

BRYCE AUSTIN

Foreword by CLIF TRIPLETT, Former Presidential Executive Fellow for Cybersecurity

TCE Strategy
www.tcestrategy.com

This book contains information obtained from authentic and well-regarded sources. Reasonable efforts have been made to validate the reliability of all data and information, but the author and publisher cannot assume responsibility for the validity of all materials or the consequences of their use. The author and publisher have attempted to track the copyright holders of all material reproduced in this publication, and apologies to copyright holders if permission to publish in this form has not been obtained. If any copyright material has not been acknowledged please let us know so we may rectify in future reprints.

Trademark notice: Product or corporate names may be trademarks or registered trademarks, and are used only for identification and explanation without intent to infringe.

Cover design and layout by Steven Plummer / spbookdesign.com

Ordering Information:
Quantity sales. Special discounts are available on quantity purchases by corporations, associations and others. For details, contact the publisher at the address above.

Library of Congress Cataloging-in-Publication Data:
Austin, Bryce—
Secure Enough? 20 Questions on Cybersecurity for Business Owners and Executives / Bryce Austin; foreword by Clifton Triplett. — 1st ed.
        p. 208 cm.
Includes bibliographical references.
ISBN 978-0-9993931-0-9 (hardback)

Visit the TCE Strategy website at https://www.tcestrategy.com
Printed in the United States of America

10 9 8 7 6 5 4 3 2 1

FREE:
PREMIUM MATERIAL

Put the lessons from this book into action immediately and ensure your business truly is "secure enough."

Download the latest checklists, case studies, and videos to share with your team, making cybersecurity a business priority and competitive advantage for your company.

DEDICATION

For Amie, Liam, Kellen, Lyrah, Ned, Alexander, Marissa, Mom and Dad. No greater gift exists than the love of family.

For Dr. Sharon Wynstra-Ballard, James L. Crow, Nancy Reese, Dr. Peter Petillo, Jerry Gray, Todd Reimringer and Todd Cohen, for your guidance, insights, and support.

ACKNOWLEDGMENTS

To an amazing group of editors/advisors: Miles Edmundson, Clif Triplett, Michael Pickard, Connie Anderson, Brian Landwehr, Barry Caplin and Gary Berman

"Gonna be a lot of roadkill on the information highway."

Greg Brown, "Whatever It Was," Slant 6 Mind. 1997

CONTENTS

FOREWORD BY CLIF TRIPLETT

SECURE ENOUGH?

SECURE *ENOUGH?* POSES questions that all senior business leaders must ask themselves. These questions are important today, and if you are not comfortable with the answers, the time for action is now. Unfortunately, cyber risk has become an inherent part of today's way of doing business. We live in digitally connected business environments. We connect to our customers, to our supply chain, and even to the machines that make, move or sell our products and services. As a business leader you should be asking yourself these questions. The book provides some very accessible information and easy-to-implement answers. You should be asking your own team the important questions at the end of each short chapter. Most likely your company has been attacked and probably breached to some degree; however, the question is: When will such a breach bring your company harm or embarrassment, or both? When that day arrives, the outside world will be asking two possibly painful questions:

1. Did this company take all the prudent and necessary actions it should have to prevent the incident from occurring?

2. How did this company react when it discovered the breach?

Secure Enough? can assist you in getting in front of these looming questions. Better yet, the vital information in it might assist you in never actually being asked.

CLIF TRIPLETT
FORMER PRESIDENTIAL EXECUTIVE FELLOW FOR CYBERSECURITY
OBAMA ADMINISTRATION

PREFACE

I WAS IN THE room when it happened.

On November 27, 2013, I was having a great Thanksgiving Day. After having dinner with my family and friends, I had the privilege of heading into work. Several projects that my teams at Target had been working on were about to be put to the test. My group managed several million dollars' worth of technology initiatives that focused on the stores themselves. Some were behind-the-scenes projects like server upgrades or new Wi-Fi systems, but others were front-and-center:

- Integration of Target.com and in-store systems to allow guests to buy an item online—and have it waiting for them at Customer Service in the store of their choice.

- The first-ever iPad application to be used by customers inside of Target stores.

- New reverse logistics systems that would save the company millions of dollars, and would also help the environment by aiding team members to properly dispose of or recycle items that could not be sold.

- New reporting systems that were used in real time by members of executive management, all the way up to the CEO.

I entered the war room on the first floor of Target City Center. The atmosphere was determined and optimistic. Over a hundred glowing computer screens stood at the ready. A small army of talented team members were lighting up systems in advance of the stores opening for business. At 3 P.M., the East Coast stores went live. Online purchases for in-store pickup began flooding in, and less than an hour later, our first in-store pickup of a Target.com purchase was completed. Everything worked as designed. Sales were strong. Issues were minimal. We had done it. I left about midnight, confident that this was a smashing success overall.

However, there was something we didn't know. We didn't know that on November 27, 2013, cybercriminals had captured thousands of our customer's credit card numbers. When the Secret Service and the FBI came knocking a few weeks later, *then we knew*. When the press broke the story, then everyone knew. Before the dust settled, tens of millions of card numbers had been stolen.

Target, like most retail stores, was investing in applications in support of more efficient store operations and enhanced customer experiences that leveraged the explosion of technology available to corporations and in the hands of consumers.

Then in a moment the world at Target and most corporations changed. The priorities shifted immediately from improving operations and generating superior customer experiences to protecting the customer and mitigating the risk now present from this new threat of cyber adversaries. Target responded as any prudent organization would, and shifted resources. The application teams were drawn down to enable a rapid increase in resources to protect their customers and the company. I had a strong background in cybersecurity from my 11 years in the financial services sector, but my role at Target focused on large customer-centric or stores-centric projects, not cybersecurity. As part of the application team, my role was eliminated to increase the budget for breach remediation.

This event shaped the next phase of my career. Preparing for cyber-attacks had a low priority for many organizations. Now it was a new reality as a major threat, and most companies were not ready to face it. I wanted to be part of this next evolution of information technology and take a thought-leadership role to assist other corporations in preparing for adversaries that were growing rapidly in numbers and sophistication. Cybercrime had become a new major revenue source for criminals and an arms race for Nation States.

Prior to my time at Target, I was in the payroll business. We were hit by cyberattacks more days than not, and we never had a serious breach. Our exposure was obvious, though. We moved money for a living. If a hacker could get in and move a bit of it for himself, it could cause enough concern with our clients that we would be out of business. A breach was simply too large of a risk to ignore, so we didn't. With a lot of hard work and a little bit of luck, we kept the cybercriminals at bay.

Cybersecurity is rarely a technology problem. It is a leadership problem. It is an executive problem.

In most businesses, that isn't the case. Cybersecurity risk is hard to understand and even harder to quantify. Budgets are tight. Technology is expensive and often difficult to implement. It's hard to convince a business owner to replace technology that still works fine for the company's needs—but has become insecure.

Why is this happening? Who are the perpetrators? Where are the failure points, and what are the most effective means of fixing them? How do we get in front of this growing crisis rather than constantly reacting to it?

What I've learned from my time in large corporations and in small/mid-sized businesses is that cybersecurity is rarely a technology problem. It's a leadership problem. It's an executive problem. Executives need to fund and support cybersecurity programs. They need to promote cyber-security best practices. They need to have cybersecurity as one of the core principles required to sustain a viable business. Cybersecurity needs to be tied to business objectives. In order to do these things, executives need to understand the fundamentals of cybersecurity. That is where this book comes in. By writing these pages, I want to:

- Help business owners and other executives understand the questions they need to ask to make good decisions about cybersecurity.

- Provide enough background on cybersecurity that you can have an intelligent conversation with a cybersecurity expert on what threats exist for your business.

- Help you understand the minimum you need to do to keep your cyber risk at a level that's acceptable to you.

INTRODUCTION

REMEMBER WHEN RADIATION made its way into the public eye around 1920? No? Well, neither do I, as none of us were around back then. It was an interesting time: a new and unique energy form was discovered. Radium was sold as a health-restoring elixir. X-rays were going to give doctors unprecedented insights into the inner workings of the human body. The future looked bright, right up until people realized that radiation caused cancer, and that there was no such thing as a minimum safe level of exposure.

There have been distinct turning-point moments in human history, such as when "germ theory" explained how to control many diseases, or how cholesterol levels helped to predict heart disease. The list goes on. All of these moments have one thing in common: the risk of radiation, germs, and cholesterol cannot be seen or felt. They cannot be easily quantified for an individual. They are difficult to understand from a visceral standpoint.

Businesses today are at a new turning point. Cybersecurity issues are making headlines around the world, impacting company reputations for years (such as Sony), changing the value and direction of businesses (Yahoo), and possibly influencing elections around the world.

This book covers none of those things. This book is about you.

You are an owner or executive in a business that is not on the Fortune 100 list. You know of others in your industry that have been hit by cybersecurity issues. If you know that there is something to be concerned about but you don't know exactly what to focus on, this book will educate you on how to close that gap.

We are going to explore the top 20 questions that every business owner or executive should be asking about their company as it relates to cybersecurity. We are going to do it with a lens that few cybersecurity professionals use: how to make a cybersecurity program part of a business plan that provides a *genuine competitive advantage* to your company. This book is not intended to teach you about every technical lesson learned, but to assist you in being active and informed so you can determine the best

It will be less expensive, less stressful and less disruptive to be proactive regarding cybersecurity.

actions to protect your company from being on the growing list of damaging breaches of cybersecurity that are highly visible. To go back to the examples of distinct turning points above, many companies use radiation to save lives every day, or to generate power that does not contribute to global warming or otherwise impact the environment (with Fukushima and Chernobyl as very notable exceptions). Government organizations use their understanding of germ theory to save countless lives. Private companies provide germ control to save lives as well, and become more profitable by doing so. Let's give your companies the competitive advantage in cybersecurity. Ask yourself and your team these 20 critical questions to gauge your current cybersecurity posture, and to get new ideas on where you want to be.

For your company, it will be less expensive, less stressful and less disruptive to be proactive regarding cybersecurity. If you are attacked, you will be working with attorneys, technology specialists and cybersecurity experts—all of whom are much more expensive than preparing your company up front to be "Secure Enough."

If some parts of this book read like a "how-to" on cybersecurity, be warned. This book only scratches the surface of these topics. Writing a book on cybersecurity is like writing a book on art. Entire library buildings could be dedicated to the topic. This book is meant to provide enough information about each area for you to ask the right questions to better prepare you to make informed and intelligent decisions.

Executives and business owners are busy people, but be assured this book will maximize your competitive advantage in a minimal amount of time. Let's get to it.

WHY IS CYBERSECURITY A PROBLEM FOR MY COMPANY?

"There are only two different types of companies in the world: those that have been breached and know it and those that have been breached and don't know it."

— TED SCHLEIN, VENTURE CAPITALIST

IT WAS UNCOMFORTABLE waiting in a Starbucks with almost $2,000 cash in my pocket. A stranger was about to walk through the front door with the expectation that I would have his money ready. He could recognize me from my LinkedIn picture, but I had only exchanged emails with him, so I was at a disadvantage.

I didn't notice her until she sat down next to me. She looked nothing like I expected, starting with her being a she. She was young, dressed in a hoodie that immediately reminded me of the TV show Mr. Robot, and she had something I needed. I needed $1870 worth of a cryptocurrency called bitcoin, and I needed it today. She didn't take the time to introduce herself.

"You're in luck," she started. "The exchange rate [of bitcoin to dollars] is down, so I'll only need $1850 from you."

"It's only 20 dollars different."

"You can pay me the full $1870 if you want."

"This is costing me too much already," I said.

"Look, I'm here to help you. It's not my fault that you're in this mess."

She was right. It wasn't her fault. The day before, I received a panicked call from one of my new clients. We had performed a cybersecurity assessment two months earlier, and we were starting down the road of developing a comprehensive cybersecurity program for them. In this case, we hadn't moved fast enough. The company's CFO had clicked on an email attachment that made its way past the malware filters, and it loaded ransomware onto his PC. It encrypted everything it could find on his hard drive, and then it went after the network shares that he had access to. In all, over 10,000 files were encrypted. The network shares were backed up the night before, so we could restore those in a matter of minutes. The hard drive in his laptop was a different story, as he had no backup. He said that several months of work was on his drive, and that if we couldn't get it back, the company's quarterly financial reports would not go out on time, which could cost the company hundreds of thousands of dollars. The $1870 in my pocket was a pittance in comparison, but my mind still bristled at the thought of giving it up to pay a ransom. But I didn't have a choice. This is what my client needed to be successful.

I handed over an envelope of cash after removing $20 from it. Ten minutes later, I was the owner of a virtual wallet that contained 4 bitcoin, which I promptly used to pay the ransom that was supposed to get my client their data back. Two hours later the keys were sent, and thankfully my client was one of the lucky ones where paying the ransom worked. They were able to unlock their data.

This client was a distributor of common commodity products. They didn't think of themselves as a high-risk target for cybercriminals. Two days earlier, they would have been right. Today, they were proven wrong.

The example above is a small one. It's one computer and a $5,000 overall loss to the company when the business disruption and consultant costs are factored in. These attacks can be much more serious, though, as the WannaCry ransomware attack of 2017 demonstrated.[1] [2] Thankfully, all but the most sophisticated ransomware attacks are easy to recover from *if cyber best practices are in place at your organization before it strikes*. If they are not, paying the ransom is often the least costly way out of the situation, which is exactly what the cybercriminals want. They create a scenario where it is cheaper to pay than deal with the consequences. Money is a common theme for cyber-crimes, and unfortunately cyber risk can manifest itself in multiple forms.

Ransomware is malicious software used to encrypt your data and demand money from you to get your data back. If the ransom is not paid, cybercriminals may delete it altogether.

Here is another example that went far beyond ransomware. It didn't make headlines, but was very important for those involved.

Negotiations had gone on for months with a prospective buyer. Acquisitions of companies on the Fortune 1000 list take time. My role was not to help them look more valuable to the prospective buyer, but rather to help interpret the results of a recent cybersecurity assessment they had undertaken. One finding was a cause of concern. Data was leaving their email server that couldn't be easily explained, and the IP addresses it was pointing to showed up on a watch list of suspected hackers' servers. Three sleepless nights later, it was conclusive:

The email server was sending the emails of several of the company's executives to a government outside of the USA that was known to engage in hacking activities. And this government was in the same country where the prospective buyer was based.

The most obvious explanation was staring us in the face, and Occam's Razor said that we had to look no further (this is a principle from philosophy: Suppose there exist two explanations for an occurrence. The simpler one is the more likely explanation). The prospective buyer had hired their government's cybersecurity team to hack the selling company and gather intelligence on the acquisition. They wanted to know what the execs were saying to each other about the purchase price and about any issues that had not been revealed over the negotiating table. It was as if the buyer had put a microphone in the office of nearly every senior leader of the company and recorded everything. Essentially, that is exactly what they did, but they never had to set foot in the company headquarters to do it. They didn't even have to step foot on USA soil. They hacked their way in and gave themselves an insurmountable advantage in the negotiations.

My client briefly talked about purposefully planting misinformation for the hackers to find, but it was too late in the process to try that now. The damage had been done, and it was unrecoverable. Negotiations were terminated. The company has not been sold. Because this cybersecurity incident never made the press, very few people heard about it. However, the major shareholders of the company who were ready to retire as very wealthy people heard about it when they learned that they would not be retiring as wealthy as anticipated.

This is the new world we live in. Cybersecurity impacts *all* companies, regardless of industry or size, because your company has money or other assets that cybercriminals perceive as easy to take. The business model for cybercriminals is too strong for it to unfold any other way. If security is not in place, you can be leveraged with cyber threats like ransomware, or damaged by the theft or corruption of your intellectual property, customer information, employee information, or financial information, each of which could cause corporate embarrassment, a loss of trust, and direct bottom line financial impact.

Until we reach a level of cybersecurity advanced enough to make these criminal acts unprofitable, attacks on vulnerable businesses and individuals will continue. Business disruptions will continue. This is why cybersecurity is a risk to every company, including yours.

QUESTIONS TO EXPLORE this topic further with your company's leaders:

> ➤ What is our liability if a cybersecurity incident causes a production outage or a data exposure?

> ➤ What regulatory concerns do we have if a breach occurs?

WHERE IS MY DATA, AND HOW CAN I KEEP IT SECURE?

"Understand what data you hold, how you are using it, and make sure that you are practicing good data hygiene."

– DAVID MOUNT, DIRECTOR, MICRO FOCUS

MANY PEOPLE HEARD about the 2014 Yahoo breach where 500 million records were stolen by hackers. Another Yahoo hack received less press, mostly because it was discovered after the 2014 breach had already made so many headlines. It turns out that in 2013, three billion (yes, three billion, as in 3,000 million—all of Yahoo's user records) were stolen from the company and posted for sale on the dark web.

The most interesting part of the 2013 breach isn't that all of Yahoo's account records were stolen or that this was "the largest known breach of a private company's computer systems," according to the New York Times.[3] It's that Yahoo and law enforcement have said nothing about how "the largest known breach of a private company's computer systems" happened. This is for one of two reasons: either they have no idea how it happened, or they do know and are still actively working the case. Either way, indictments have already been handed down regarding the 2014 hack of 500 million records. As a result, the three-billion-record hack remains even more interesting.

One thing is for certain: Someone had access to that data and illegally made a copy of it.

- Was that access from the production systems that were supposed to house it?

- Was it from a backup copy of that data?

- Was it from a test or development system that was using live data instead of dummy data?

As of this writing several years later, we simply don't know.

The Yahoo story demonstrates another important point: Stealing data is very different than stealing money or other tangible objects. The theft of tangible objects is a zero-sum game: if something is stolen from you, the thief now has that thing and you do not. This is how Fort Knox works: Keep others from stealing the gold. Stealing sensitive data or intellectual property doesn't work that way. Whoever gets unauthorized access to your data can do many different things with it, all of which will cause harm to your company. They can:

1. Copy it and use it for their own purposes. This is what allegedly happened to DuPont with their titanium dioxide refining process.[4] [5]

2. Sell it on the black market, causing you damage in several ways: financial, reputational, and perhaps even criminal liability. The Home Depot and Anthem breaches are great examples.[6] [7]

3. Encrypt your data and try to force you to pay them to get it back. This is how the ransomware business model works.[1] [2]

4. Edit your data without your knowledge, causing you to make the wrong decisions for your company as a result of looking at data that you thought was accurate but instead had been deliberately manipulated. These are called "data-integrity attacks," and are among the most difficult kind of cyber-attacks to detect.[8]

In order to protect your data against any of the above issues, you must first identify where your data is located, and who has what level of access to it. Start your cybersecurity journey there. If Sweden had properly gone through this process, there would have been far fewer headlines in the summer of 2017 about them allowing improper access to life-and-death information, such as the names of the people in their witness protection program.[9] [10]

Finding all your data is substantially harder than it sounds. Imagine that someone took a 1,000-piece puzzle and scattered it around every nook and cranny of your home. Most of the pieces will be obvious to find, some will be more challenging, and some will be nearly impossible. However, the 1,000-piece puzzle analogy has a key difference than your data search has: it's easy to tell when you are missing a puzzle piece. That is not

Finding all your data is substantially harder than it sounds.

the case when you are searching for your data. It is important to keep in mind that just because you think you have identified the locations of your data, it doesn't mean you really have. Even if you did find it all, it doesn't mean that tomorrow there won't be a large copy of your data somewhere that wasn't there today. This is an ongoing process, and it isn't going to be perfect. That's okay, though—this exercise will still be very valuable, and later in this book, you will see ways to protect yourself regarding the puzzle pieces you miss.

Step 1: Make a list of all applications used in your company. This is a more challenging exercise than you may think. The proliferation of cloud services has made every user a potential source of a new application. However, valuable insights can be had here.

- What if the top 10% of your salespeople are using a tracking tool that the others aren't?

- What if you have so many people using a niche subscription product for your industry that signing a master agreement (at a substantial discount) will save you a lot of money in the long term?

- What if that fancy Customer Relationship Management (CRM) system is used by less than half of the people that were supposed to be using it, and perhaps it should be retired altogether?

Understanding the applications your business uses will lead to a better understanding of your business as a whole.

Step 2: List the type of data held in each application. You may need to make some guesses here, as it's nearly impossible to know what people put into the "notes" field of an application. Normally, a reasonable picture can be made of what type of data sits where.

Step 3: Find file shares on your network where people store data that isn't associated with a centralized application. A "file share" is exactly what it sounds like: it is a part of your network where multiple people can access the same files. Normally they hold files such as Word documents, PDF files or Excel spreadsheets. Tools are available that can help with this search, and many of them can also scan your company's desktops and laptops.

Step 4: Categorize the different types of data by how important they are to your company, and/or how valuable they are to cybercriminals (or to your competitors).

Step 5: Look for copies of your information outside of the primary systems designed to house it. Technology exists to search through all of your data files to identify particular data types. A manual search is generally too time consuming and highly inaccurate. An experienced cybersecurity consultant can help you with this process.

Let's start with how valuable your files are to cybercriminals. Data generally falls into four categories: 1) Publicly Available, 2) Sensitive, 3) Confidential, and 4) Top Secret. Let's define these in a bit more detail.

TOP SECRET DATA

Top Secret data is the most important data to keep from those that would use it to take away your competitive advantage. Here is a list of sample data types that generally fall into the top-secret category:

- Critical intellectual property your company owns. The recipe for Coca-Cola is a good example.[11]

- Usernames and passwords for your systems.

- Any biometric ID data or other multi-factor authentication system. Remember the OPM breach?[12] If not, Google it—over 5 million fingerprints were stolen because they were stored in an unencrypted database. It's hard to issue someone a new set of fingerprints.

- Upcoming merger and acquisition activities that your company is investigating.

- Research and development projects (depending on the potential competitive advantage the product or service you are developing is to your company).

- Credit card numbers when stored with the card's pin, expiration date, zip code where the bill is delivered, or the name of the cardholder.

- Any list of known vulnerabilities in your physical or cybersecurity programs.

- Encryption certificates.

- Any data that, if disclosed, could pose a life-safety concern (this is rare, but it was true of the USA's Office of Personnel Management (OPM) breach).[12]

- Source code. Source code is a term for computer programs in the format that programmers use to write programs in. Source code that your company writes is top secret for any program that handles any of the data described above, even if that data is fully encrypted. If a hacker has access to your source code, they often can break your encryption (look up *memory scraping* online for more details). The value of source code is often overlooked, and has been directly responsible for large security breaches.

Thankfully, the procedure on what to do with **Top Secret data** is the easiest to describe: protect it as if your company's survival depends on it, because in reality, it does.

- Include in your employee training an understanding of top-secret data and how to handle it.

- Limit access to those with a genuine need to know.

- Limit permissions of those with access to have the least access that they need in order to do their job. For example, the list of those who can edit data should be smaller than the list of those who can read it. The list of who can give others access to it should be the smallest of all.

- Remember that anyone with access to this data can copy it in some way. Even if you lock down the ability to copy the data, print the data, or email the data, how are you going to stop someone from taking a picture of their computer monitor with their smartphone?

- Encrypt this data whenever it is in motion.

- Encrypt this data at rest (while it is sitting on a server, on a desktop/laptop, or on a USB drive).

- Encrypt the backups of this data. *Remember that anyone with access to the backups has access to your top-secret data.*

- Isolate the servers that contain this data as much as possible from the rest of your network. The concepts of a network "DeMilitarized Zone (DMZ)", or even better, a "zero-trust network"[13] [14] are very useful in keeping cybercriminals away from this data. More on these in Question 16, section 12.

- Employ an auditing system to track every time someone reads or changes this data. Treat the auditing system itself as top secret.

Top-secret data is the information that could cause serious harm to your company if it falls into the wrong hands. As long as you understand what data should be in this category, and are taking steps to keep it safe, you are already ahead of the game.

CONFIDENTIAL DATA

Let's move onto confidential data. This is the type of data that would cause business disruption or damage to its reputation if it were to be made public. Confidential data is often what we think of when we hear about a data breach in the news. The Anthem breach (80 million health records stolen) is a good example.[7]

Typical examples of this type of data include:

- Bank account numbers.

- Credit card numbers when stored without pin numbers, expiration dates, etc.

- Social Security numbers (SSNs).

- Healthcare information, also called PHI (protected by HIPAA).
  NOTE: some companies put SSNs and PHI into the Top Secret category.

- Employee salary and other HR information.

- Upcoming layoffs or other significant organizational changes.

- Financial information about your company that is not generally publicly available.

- Your intellectual property that is not so critical that it falls into the Top Secret category.

- Discussions of legal cases, etc. (e.g. items tagged "Attorney/ Client Privilege").

- Any source code your company writes, when the type of data the program handles is not considered top secret. Again, source code is far more valuable than many companies believe it to be.

Confidential data has a similar set of *best practices* as does Top Secret, but generally those practices are not taken to the same extreme:

- Include in your employee training an understanding of confidential data and how to handle it.

- Limit access to those with a genuine need to know.

- Limit permissions of those with access to have the least access that they need in order to do their job.

- Remember that anyone with access to this data can copy it in some way.

- Encrypt this data whenever it is in motion.

- Encrypt this data at rest whenever it is outside of a datacenter. Laptops can be stolen. Smartphones can be stolen. Make sure that when a laptop is stolen from your company, the extent of the loss is only the replacement value of the laptop.

- Encrypt the backups of this data. Remember that anyone with access to the backups has access to your confidential data.

SENSITIVE DATA

Okay, we are through the really damaging information types. Let's talk about Sensitive data. Sensitive information is the kind of data that your company does not want to be publicly available, but it isn't going to make the front page of a major news site if it does. This typically includes data such as:

- A list of your employees.

- Non-publicly available phone numbers.

- A list of your customers.

- Sales performance numbers (this could be Confidential if your company is publicly traded).

- Prices you are paying for raw materials.

- Open job positions you have not yet posted.

Sensitive information is the kind of data where the efficiency of your company must be weighed against the expense of putting strong security measures into place. Regarding the treatment of sensitive data, my recommendations are simple: pick and choose the *best practices* from the list above that your risk tolerance and budget will allow. Not sure which ones make sense? Here is what I recommend:

- Include in your employee training an understanding of sensitive data and how to handle it.

- Limit access to this data to those that need it to do their jobs.

- Encrypt your laptops.

- Encrypt your backups.

PUBLICLY AVAILABLE DATA

Finally, Publicly Available data. Publicly available information about your company is usually the kind of information you *want* out in the public domain. In fact, you may be paying people to help get it out there. Items like the products and services you provide, your physical locations, hours of operation, phone numbers, your current advertisements, and the like are all publicly available information.

Generally speaking, you have no cybersecurity risk with this type of information. That being said, remember that cybercriminals often use scams to trick your employees to give up information from the other three categories, and that your publicly available information may be a way that they trick someone into sharing information they shouldn't or behaving in a way that they shouldn't. It is important that your cybersecurity awareness training program include lessons for your employees to understand how publicly available information can be used both to your advantage, and to your detriment.

Furthermore, most publicly available information about your company did not start out as publicly available. Before you buy a new building to house a new branch of your company, information about the upcoming sale is normally considered confidential. Before you launch a new product with a massive advertising campaign, information about that product is often top secret. Data has a life cycle where it can move from one category to the other.

Before any new system is developed, it is critical to answer the type of data it will contain, who should have access to it, and what the life cycle of that data might be.

Before any new system is developed, it is critical to answer the type of data it will contain, who should have access to it, and what the life cycle of that data might be.

In summary, finding your data is pivotal to protecting it. In order to consider this section complete, you should have compiled a list of the following:

- The applications your company uses.

- The type of data stored in each application.

- The level of confidentiality of each type of data (top secret, confidential, sensitive, or publicly available).

- The network shares that store data that isn't associated with a centralized application.

- The groups of users that have access to each data store, the level of access they have, *and the business reason they have that type of access.*

- The method that each data share is backed up, if those backups are well protected, and who has the ability to restore them.

If this sounds overwhelming, do not worry. Outside consulting companies can lead exercises like this. They will know the right questions to ask your team members so that all the nooks and crannies where your data is hiding are discovered.

After this has been completed, someone needs to take responsibility for the maintenance and upkeep of this list of what type of data sits where. More about this in the section for Question 6: *Where does the buck stop for cybersecurity concerns at my company?*

We have addressed the levels of sensitivity of data in your company. Let's shift gears to how important various data stores are to your company (per step 4 above). This is generally easier to answer than the level of confidentiality of your data. I recommend that my clients rate their data by answering a single question: **How long can you go without access to it?**

- If you can't operate normal business functions for even one hour without a certain data store, then it should be in the "mission critical" category.

- If you can go up to one business day without a certain data source, then it is in the "very important" category.

- If you can go for up to a week without a data source, then it is "important."

- If you can go for more than a week, then that data falls into the "deferrable" category.

I realize that this is a simplistic view, as it doesn't take into account things like critical research and development projects that have not yet seen the light of day, but you are banking your company's future on them. Bear with me here. I promised that this book would be sensitive of your available time, and of course there will be exceptions to the categories above. Use good judgment on how important data is to the current and future status of your company, and treat that data appropriately. The fact that you are going through this exercise already puts you ahead of much of your competition.

Finding and securing your data is a cornerstone of your cybersecurity program. When this exercise is complete, your team should have:

- A complete inventory of your applications.

- A complete inventory of your data stores.

- A categorization of the type and sensitivity of data in each data store.

- A list of which job functions need a specific level of access to each data store and why.

- An owner of each data store who can make decisions on permissions to that data.

QUESTIONS TO EXPLORE this topic further with your company's leaders:

➤ What sensitive data does your department create, consume, and store?

➤ What protections exist to keep that data secure?

➤ Who determines where your department's data sits, both inside the company and outside?

➤ Who determines who gets access to which data?

HOW VALUABLE A TARGET IS MY COMPANY TO CYBERCRIMINALS?

"There was this horrible moment where I realized there was absolutely nothing at all that I could do."
— AMY PASCAL, FORMER CEO OF SONY PICTURES

THE WORST DATA breach in healthcare history was the Anthem breach of February 2015. More than 78.8 million records were stolen by a Nation State that does not have strong diplomatic relations with the USA. Those records included the names, birth dates, Social Security numbers, and home addresses of the individuals that ever did business with Anthem—or even applied for a policy.[7][15]

Some companies know they are in the crosshairs of the best cybercriminals in the world.

- Do you have a large store of HIPAA data that would be worth serious money on the dark web?

- Do you process over one million credit card transactions per year? People on the dark web would pay handsomely for your customers' credit card numbers.

- Are you in the payroll or money-transfer business?

- Are you developing a technology that foreign governments would be interested in?

- Are you in a business that a hacktivist group or Nation State may find ethically questionable?

If you can answer yes to any of the above questions, congratulations, you are in the highest-risk group. If you are in this group and you can't easily answer all 20 questions in this book, I hope you have a strong cybersecurity insurance policy.

Most companies are not in the highest-risk category. For the rest of us, companies fall into three large groups, including those that have:

- A significant regulatory environment to operate within (healthcare, banking, insurance, etc.).

- Data that others could monetize (trade secrets, credit card numbers, Personally Identifiable Information (PII), financial data on publicly traded companies that has not yet been made public, etc.).

- Data that is important and necessary for the company to operate (that's the rest of us).

If I had written this book before the proliferation of ransomware, I would not have included the third category. In fact, I used to lambast salespeople selling cybersecurity tools that said, "Everyone is a target." The problem is that cybercriminals have figured out an important new angle to their business model: companies that don't have information that is valuable on the black market still have information *that's valuable to the company itself.* The bad guys are finding a way into a company, encrypting as much data as possible, and then extorting money from you to get your own data back.

It's a very profitable business, so much so that companies have sprung up offering "ransomware as a service" for those that want to be cyber-criminals but don't have the technical expertise to do the job themselves. It's rather disgusting for those of us that are in the business of helping companies avoid cybercriminals, but it's reality.

Welcome to the modern business environment. Ransomware is growing at an amazing rate: in 2016 alone, the frequency of successful ransomware attacks doubled against consumers and tripled against businesses.[16]

The reality of today's world is that we are all targets. From hospitals that need their Enterprise Resource Planning (ERP) system to treat patients, to accounting firms that need their tax engine software to process their clients' tax returns, to the San Francisco Municipal transit system, every company wants to prevent business disruptions. Ransomware attacks are designed to disrupt your company's ability to do business *until you pay up*. This unfortunate truth is one of the motivators that prompted me to write this book. Cybersecurity is now everyone's problem, and education about cybersecurity is one of the best weapons we have in order to fight back.

Determining your value to a cybercriminal is as much art as science. There is a classic equation to determine risk, but I include it only as a reference point:

Actual damages from a breach, multiplied by the probability that a breach will occur = TOTAL RISK

I'm often asked, "How can I assess my actual risk?" While the above equation is an interesting place to start, the truth is that you don't. This is similar to assessing your risk of contracting a certain disease or of having a tornado damage your home. These things happen rarely, and as such, it's impossible to say that a given company will experience a cybersecurity incident of X dollars in total damage every Y years. A better plan of attack is the following:

1. Accept that your company is a target of cybercriminals that would hope to profit from your success, either by stealing

your valuable information, or by encrypting your valuable information and ransoming it back to you. The fact that you are reading this book probably means you already understand this and are working to adapt your business model to this new reality.

2. Assess your relative risk. The areas to take into account include company size, industry, the number of countries you do business in (especially those known to support state-sponsored hacking), and the cybersecurity countermeasures you employ. I could write a whole book on this one topic, so consider this area one that deserves a "deep dive" at a later date.

3. Assess your own risk tolerance, assess the potential damage to your company that a hacker could inflict, and assess what cybersecurity countermeasures you currently have employed. Countermeasures include many of the topics in this book, and if you employ them, your risk will be far lower than many of your competitors, even if putting an actual number on it is challenging.

One of the best ways to quantify your cybersecurity risk is to get quotes for cybersecurity insurance. The cost of insurance says a lot about the real risk that your company has for breaches that cause real damage to your company. As an example, I was shocked when I received a few quotes on automobile insurance to learn that my wife's large pickup truck was less than half the cost to insure than my sports car, even though her truck was worth more than three times what my car was. My insurance carrier explained it this way: the type of car you drive plays a huge role in your insurance rates. Simply put, some cars get into more accidents than others, some are stolen more often than others, some are more expensive to fix than others, and in some, it's more likely you will be injured in them than others. All those factors are taken into account when a policy price is determined, and it pays to drive a vehicle with low insurance rates.

Let's put this into a business setting. If your building's fire insurance policy costs $10,000 per year for $1 million in coverage, then the insurance company thinks you will have a large claim on that policy less than once every 100 years. Otherwise they would lose money selling you the policy. In fact, they are probably guessing that you will have a large fire once every 500 years so that they make a good profit on the policy. If it costs $250,000 for the same coverage, your risk of having a fire is much higher than that. The cost of a cybersecurity insurance policy will help you determine the relative risk of a cyber incident in comparison to another type of business incident, such as a building issue (fire/flood), an operational issue (the loss of a key executive in your company), or a liability issue of some sort.

Another lens that is helpful to gauge your real risk of cybercrime is to determine how many different types of cybercriminals would be interested in hacking you. Question 4 focuses on that very topic.

In summary, your company is at risk of cyberattack if a criminal believes there is a good return to be had on their investment of time and money. If your defenses are poor, then the effort they have to put in is low. If you have strong defenses then the return must be high for the adversary to expend significant resources to try to breach your systems. Many attacks are non-specific. They search for a particular vulnerability across many companies and report back success. This is known as reconnaissance. If you are found to be vulnerable, you will probably be attacked. Criminals will try to monetize their efforts in many ways. Your data is valuable to you, and they can monetize this via ransomware. Cybercriminals normally put ransom requests around $500 for individuals and $20,000 to $150,000 for corporations.[16] Your data may be valuable to cybercriminals because they can use it themselves or sell it to others. Your data could be a very serious liability if improper disclosure of that data violates laws such as HIPAA (See Question 9). Large data breaches can cost millions (See Question 10). Pricing on a cybersecurity insurance policy is a good start to quantify your cyber risk relative to other insurable risks.

QUESTIONS TO EXPLORE this topic further with your company's leaders:

➤ Who in our industry has been hit by cybersecurity incidents?

➤ What commodity data do we possess that is valuable on the black market?

➤ What is the total value of our data if it were to hit the dark web?

➤ How much would we be willing to pay if someone was to shut down our business with a cyberattack?

WHO ARE THESE CYBERCRIMINALS?

"Instead of focusing on the #malware, focus on the cyber-attacker. He is greedy, he has weaknesses and he makes mistakes."

— SHLOMO TOUBOL, CEO OF ILLUSIVE NETWORKS

WHEN I WAS in high school, computer networks were just entering the mainstream educational system. I enjoyed learning about them. I used to sell computers at Best Buy, and worked on networks at small businesses in my spare time. Cybersecurity was a genuine concern even back then. Computer systems were being used for sensitive purposes, such as tracking grades or recording student absences (remember the famous scene from *Ferris Bueller's Day Off*?). My senior year of high school, I had an interesting proposition from my English teacher: obtain the network password of the computer teacher at our school and give it to her. She said that the computer teacher had bragged about how his network was "hack proof," and she wanted to challenge that assumption. This sounded like fun, and I wanted to learn more about cybersecurity.

Challenge accepted.

I had two large problems: One, if I genuinely tried to break into the school computer system by hooking up my own computer and using hacking tools, I may cause problems for the operations of the school, and I wasn't willing to do that (not to mention the whole "expulsion from school and don't get your high school diploma" issue). Two, I had no idea where to start. I didn't know Novell networks as well as I knew Windows, and even if I did, I was not part of the team that had any level of access to them. At first, I thought this whole idea was over before it started.

Then a good friend offered a different way to look at this issue: I want to get the computer teacher's password, and not get caught doing it. That's it. This isn't an advanced hack. All I need is to find someone that can look over his shoulder when he logs in. I approached another friend who had two classes with the computer teacher, and he was able to see the first two keystrokes that the teacher typed in. Not much to go on, but it was something. I did a bit of digging to find out the names of his close family members, his pets, the kind of car he drove, and so on. I also found out that the network was set up to allow for 10 password attempts before locking a user out, which meant I had nine guesses before giving up. Those first two characters of his password were a key advantage. I could eliminate all but two of the possibilities I developed using that information. I got it on the second guess: it was his middle name. I proudly walked in to my English teacher's classroom, handed her a small piece of paper with his password on it, and walked out. I was so proud of it that I'm surprised my head fit through the doorway. To be honest, ego is what drove many hackers of that era.

Does that make me a cybercriminal? Technically speaking, yes. I logged into a system using a username and password that was not assigned to me. However, my intent was to help my English teacher display that there was a need for better security measures in the school's computer system, rather than to exploit this vulnerability for my own gain. That is the definition of a "white-hat" hacker.

The era of the '90s hacker is long since over. Today's hackers are in the game for much more practical motivations:

1. Profit. They want money and you have information they can monetize.

2. Influence. You have information they can use to manipulate business or personal situations in their favor.

3. Power. You are a government or a large corporation that controls a country, dominates an industry, or owns critical resources. Others wish to take that power away from you and use it for their own advantage. Hackers help them accomplish that goal.

Motives such as these change the way cybercriminals operate. They are organized. They share information amongst each other. The government they work for often protects them. They are well funded. These things make them more dangerous.

Who are today's cybercriminals? Let's break it down:

Individual hackers. Ever heard of Frank Abagnale? While Frank was not a cybercriminal, he was the predecessor of the modern hacker. The movie *Catch Me If You Can* was all about him. He later became a security consultant, but in his youth (ages 15–21) he was a confidence trickster, check forger, and imposter pretending he had many skills and 8 personalities—like pilot, lawyer, USA Federal agent, etc.

What about Kevin Mitnick? Kevin rose to fame a few decades ago when his hacking activities into companies like Motorola made worldwide headlines. He was arrested and spent 5 years in prison (including 8 months in solitary confinement) as a result. Hackers like this are still around, but for the most part, this type of cybercrime is long over. It's simply too profitable to employ others into a criminal enterprise of cybercrime. For those of us trying to fight them, this is a bad turn of affairs. Hackers like Kevin

Mitnick hacked because they could. They hacked for the challenge of it. Breaking into computer systems was their version of climbing Mt. Everest.

Nation States. Every major (and most minor) government has had active espionage programs in place as far back in history as anyone cares to remember. This is nothing new. What is new is the level of sophistication of their hacking capabilities, and the partnership between private companies and government organizations to commit hacks against other organizations (or other Nation States). To be blunt, if a foreign government wants to hack your organization, they will likely succeed. It's simply a matter of the amount of effort they must go through to do it, and whether or not their activities will be detected. Thankfully, for the majority of companies, foreign governments are not interested in hacking you. While attribution on who committed an attack is difficult, there are major cyber incidents where private entities were likely targeted by a Nation State, such as the Sony Pictures breach of 2014.[17] There are also examples of private companies getting caught in the cyber crossfire between Nation States, such as the large law firm DLA Piper's serious systems outage as a result of the destructive virus targeted at the Ukraine in 2017 called "Petya" or "NotPetya" by the media.[18][19] If you do business in a country that is known to support such activities, you should consider your company (and yourself) a high-risk target.

Organized crime. Organized crime has intelligent people as part of their organization. Instead of using their power for the light side of the Force, they have fallen victim to the dark side... They look for low-risk, high-reward activities to fund their enterprises, and cybercrime is one of those activities. The odds of being caught are low. The ability to monetize their activities is getting easier every day. These people work with a disregard for the rule of law, and as such, they look for opportunities to make a buck without concern for the disruption it causes others. If your company is deemed an easy target, you may be infiltrated by an organized cyber-crime operation. The trick here is to make your company slightly more difficult to break into than your peers. This is the "porcupine" approach to cybersecurity. If a wolf catches a porcupine, he has a potential meal, but getting to that meal is noticeably harder than if the wolf catches a squirrel. Don't be a squirrel.

Hacktivists. If you have heard of Anonymous, you know who hacktivists are. Other than Nation States, hacktivists are the last holdout of cybercriminals that are not in it for the money. They are in it because they believe that they are "serving the greater good" by making it harder for your company to do business. Hacktivism can take many forms, and different people will classify hacktivist differently depending on their point of view. Was the Ashely Madison breach hacktivism or run-of-the-mill hacking? Your view probably depends on whether your spouse had an account at this Canadian online dating service. Was the cyberweapon that took out Iran's plutonium centrifuges, Stuxnet, an act of hacktivism?[20] [21] [22] Depends on whom you ask, and on your opinion of nuclear proliferation. It is left as an exercise for the reader to make your own judgment here, but the bottom line is that some cybercriminals still do what they do for reasons other than money. If you are in a line of business that someone or some government may consider to be unsavory, hacktivism is a genuine threat to your organization.

The problem with hacktivists is that they are going after your company in particular. They are not targeting your whole industry or companies that leave themselves exposed and are "low-hanging fruit." That's what the hackers that are after profit go for. Hacktivists choose their targets for a specific reason, the same way that the movie *Super Size Me* chose to target McDonalds. McDonalds is the biggest company in the fast food industry, and that movie was designed to expose the health concerns of fast food.

Hacktivists want to disrupt your business's ability to conduct business, and in that regard, they are similar to Nation State attacks. Strong defenses are required if you are a target of hacktivists. Thankfully, the funding behind their efforts normally pales compared to a Nation State.

Your own employees. This is a difficult topic. While it's true that internal employees are responsible for a large number of cybersecurity breaches, it's also true that most of these are unintentional.[23] They are a result of good people doing something they shouldn't, either out of ignorance or because a cybercriminal tricked them into doing it (think Frank Abagnale social-engineering behavior). Statistics on the exact percentage of "insider" cyber breaches that are deliberate vs. inadvertent vary widely,[24] [25] but I am of the opinion that the vast majority of insider threats are *not* malicious. No matter which statistic you believe, everyone agrees that many insider threats would have been prevented if the insider had understood how his or her behavior allowed a breach to occur. It's easy to see why a good cybersecurity awareness training program is so important to the success of your company.

If your company is one of the unlucky ones where an insider deliberately caused a security breach, then you are automatically in the highest risk category of those susceptible to cybercrime. The keys to mitigate this risk are simple:

- Establish a strong cybersecurity awareness training program for your employees.

- Perform background checks on your employees to assist in identifying those that may take deliberate actions that would harm your company.

- Limit your employees' ability to obtain access (intentional or unintentional) to sensitive information via a least-privileged approach to your data.

- Remove "local administrator privileges" from your users to their company-provided laptops or desktops. A "local administrator" is someone who can do anything he chooses to with a computer, such as install programs, delete files, change sensitive security settings, and so on.

More on local administrators in Question 16, Section 5.

Thieves come in many forms, including those that:

- Work for large organized crime syndicates.
- Are one-man bands trying to make a profit.
- Are part of a government that doesn't like your organization.
- Have a value system that believes that the business you are in is somehow immoral.

Thankfully, these groups tend to use the same techniques to get into your systems. The biggest differentiators between them are the complexity of their attacks and their level of determination and patience to achieve their goal. Now that we know who these cybercriminals are, let's shift gears to discuss whose responsibility it is to fight them.

QUESTIONS TO EXPLORE this topic further with your company's leaders:

➤ Is our organization a target for Nation State level attacks? Are we part of critical infrastructure, are we known as a leader in our industry, or are we in a type of business that other countries may object to?

➤ Do we do business in a country where we may be caught in the crossfire of Nation State attacks?

WHY ISN'T LAW ENFORCEMENT DOING MORE ABOUT CYBERCRIME? WHY IS THIS MY PROBLEM?

"As the world is increasingly interconnected, everyone shares the responsibility of securing cyberspace."

– NEWTON LEE, AUTHOR OF *COUNTERTERRORISM AND CYBERSECURITY: TOTAL INFORMATION AWARENESS*

YOU AND I live in a house with windows. Windows are nice. They let in light, they make rooms feel more, well, "roomy" than they actually are, and on days with good weather, letting in a fresh breeze always feels good. Windows have three down sides: They are expensive to build compared with a normal wall, they are expensive to maintain and may need periodic replacement, and they are a genuine security risk. Throwing a rock through a window is easy to do, and would cause a genuine disruption to the day-to-day workings of your home. Taken to the extreme, throwing a Molotov cocktail or firing a rifle through a window at a target inside your home is also easy to do. Why in the world would anyone *ever* take such risks? Because we have the rule of law, that's why. Overall, the police do a good job enforcing laws that protect us against crimes of violence, and because of it, we as a society are willing to accept the risk of having windows in our homes. Furthermore, in order to commit one of the crimes I just mentioned, *the criminal has to be physically outside my home*. That is a huge deterrent in and of itself.

Today there are just over 7 billion people in the world. If we assume that 7000 people live or work close enough to you to try to throw a rock through your window, that means that 99.9999% of everyone in the world is *not* in a position to do so. For those that are close enough, the prospect of being caught, prosecuted, and punished for such behavior is an effective deterrent.

That is why we are okay having windows in our homes.

Now let's move onto the cyberworld. Remember the whole premise that "the criminal has to be outside my window to commit a crime"? Well, that kind of thinking is out the window when it comes to cybercrime (pun fully intended). People in any country anywhere in the world can be outside any cyber window, and they can test what sorts of rocks they can throw at it anytime they want. They are often located in countries where the laws of your country do not apply, and their country may not have an agreement, called a Mutual Legal Assistance Treaty (MLAT), with your country's government to prosecute crimes across borders.

With that context in mind, it's pretty obvious that law enforcement is at a serious disadvantage when it comes to cybercrime. Law enforcement can't prosecute many of these crimes. Even when they can, finding the real perpetrator of the crime is very challenging. The sheer volume of cybercrimes being committed is daunting, and appears to be growing exponentially.[26] Until a worldwide agreement exists on what is and is not lawful behavior on the Internet, it is up to you to make your company more difficult to hack into than other companies of your size in your industry.

The truth is that law enforcement is doing a lot to protect companies against cybercrime. While you now understand why their powers are limited by legal, logistical, and technical constraints, that doesn't mean that law enforcement isn't keeping the cyber world much safer than it otherwise would be. My perspective is from a standpoint of the USA because that is where I live. Your country will have a similar list.

Here are some of the things that law enforcement does for us:

- Prosecute cybercriminals in the USA and in countries with a Mutual Legal Assistance Treaty with the USA.[27]

- Facilitate partnerships between the government and private-sector companies (see info on Infragard below).

- Provide specialized cybersecurity services to companies under attack from cybercriminals, as well as educate companies on cyber safety.[28]

How does this apply to your company? Simple: you don't know when you will need law enforcement's help, so develop a relationship with them before you need them. Understand the services that they can provide to help you. The local Secret Service head of Orlando, Florida, explained it best to me: "When is it easier to exchange business cards: over coffee or over a crime scene?" Contacting them is easier than you may think, and the citations in this section will lead you to websites with their contact information.

1. Reach out to your regional Department of Homeland Security (DHS) representative. This person may be geographically farther from you than other government branches (they only have 10 regional offices for 50 states).[28]

   Part of the role of the DHS is to actively help companies detect, mitigate and prevent cybercrime. **There is a very important law passed by the USA government in late 2015 known as the Cyber Act. It states that, "Liability protections are provided to entities that voluntarily share and receive cyber threat indicators and defensive measures with other entities or the government."**[29]

I have spoken with individuals that hold or have held prominent positions in the government, and I'm told the Cyber Act allows you to volunteer cybersecurity information to the DHS and remain immune from criminal prosecution. The DHS is available to help keep your company safe.

2. Reach out to your local Secret Service representative if you handle credit cards.[30] They handle crimes that impact the value of US currency, and credit card fraud falls into that category.

3. Reach out to your local FBI cybercrime representative if you have sensitive data outside of credit cards.[31] While the FBI leans toward attribution and prosecution of cybercriminals, they are still a valuable resource to you in the event of a cyber emergency.

4. If you perform a function that is critical infrastructure for our society (power generation, water or sewer services, financial services, transportation, etc.), look for an Infragard group to join in your area.[32] Infragard is a partnership between the FBI and members of the private sector. Its goal is to protect the vital services that we depend on. See the footnote for their website on where chapters are located and how to join one.

5. Are you in any of the following industries? Automotive, Aviation, Communications, Industrial Supply Chain, Defense Contractor, Oil/Natural Gas Production/Distribution, Electricity Production/Distribution, Medical Crisis Services (first responders), Financial Services, Healthcare Supply Chain, HealthCare Provider, Information Technology, Maritime Services (ocean carriers, cruise lines, port facilities, etc.), Government

Organizations, Real Estate, Higher Education, Retail, Supply Chain Logistic Services, Ground Transportation, or Water. If so, there is an ISAC (Information Sharing and Analysis Center) specifically for your industry. These organizations exist solely to aid companies like yours to understand the cybersecurity landscape of your specific industry, to exchange best practices on cyber defense, and to exchange active intelligence on current cyberthreats.[33] Join your industry's ISAC.

The bottom line is that law enforcement is doing a lot to help protect us from cybercrime, but they have a tough job to do, and an even tougher job bringing the cybercriminals to justice. Now we know who these cybercriminals are (from Question 4) and why law enforcement is at such a disadvantage when it comes to bringing them to justice. Let's shift gears to identifying the person responsible for cybersecurity for your organization.

QUESTIONS TO EXPLORE this topic further with your company's leaders:

➤ Do we know our Federal and local representatives for cybercrime prevention?

➤ What is our policy on when we reach out to these agencies? Who has the authority to make that decision?

WHO IS RESPONSIBLE FOR CYBERSECURITY CONCERNS AT MY COMPANY?

"You have to make sure it is your boss who gets fired."
– DINIS CRUZ, OPEN WEB APPLICATION SECURITY PROJECT

THE FACT THAT many large retailers did not have a designated Chief Information Security Officer (CISO) was a large issue in the media reports of recent retail breaches. It may have contributed to the ease with which some of these hacks were performed. Legislation is now working to fill this gap in certain industries by mandating that a CISO be a *named individual* within companies. Some legislation, such as General Data Protection Regulation (GDPR) in Europe, requires that a position of Data Protection Officer exist as well. Large corporations have been under fire for not having a designated CISO as part of their executive leadership team. Not having a CISO role in your organization can negatively impact

Large corporations have been under fire for not having a designated CISO as part of their executive leadership team.

you at many angles: From genuine cybersecurity breaches, to a poor response to a breach, to negative press about the lack of this function. From a financial reporting standpoint, the Sarbanes-Oxley (SOX) act requires accurate and transparent financial reporting of USA-based companies, and being able to prove that financial records have not been tampered with is an important piece of meeting those requirements.[34] SOX and cybersecurity are joined at the hip in that regard.

If you are a business owner or executive, you already know that tying a person's compensation to his performance is part of getting good results from your employees. This is what commissioned sales is all about. Most companies have someone who oversees sales; someone who heads operations, someone who leads finance, and someone who manages HR. Even if you don't have specific individuals assigned solely to those functions, certain people are responsible for them. If sales are down, you know whom to speak with to devise a plan of attack, plain and simple.

Cybersecurity is a responsibility that spans all aspects of a company. Depending on the size of your organization, you might have in-house legal counsel, or you might outsource that function in the form of an attorney-on-retainer. You might have a head of IT, or you might outsource that as well to a managed services provider. An in-house or outsourced approach is okay, as long as those resources are available to you when you need them.

Cybersecurity is a responsibility that spans all aspects of a company. If someone needs technology to do his or her job, that person needs to have a basic understanding of cybersecurity. Who is responsible for the cybersecurity aspects of your organization? Does that person's job description include a bonus plan for meeting certain previously agreed upon cybersecurity goals for your company, such as meeting PCI compliance guidelines, becoming ISO 27001 certified, or meeting GDPR requirements? If you don't know what those acronyms mean, don't worry about it. You are a business owner or executive, and getting too far into the weeds on cybersecurity is unproductive.

However, you must have someone as part of your core team who knows those acronyms inside and out. It is okay if that person is in-house or out-sourced. Various firms specialize in providing advisory services to businesses that need a CISO, but not on a full-time basis.

How do you fix this issue? Create the role of Chief Information Security Officer in your organization. Decide if this is a full-time or part-time position. Finding someone who genuinely understands your organization's competitive advantages is critical. There is no "one-size-fits-all" solution to cybersecurity, and if implemented in a manner that causes a poor end-user experience, cybersecurity can do more harm than good to the bottom line of your organization.

It is critical to find a CISO that can help you understand the minimum you need to do to reduce your cybersecurity risk to a level that is acceptable to you. This person should understand your industry and your business well enough to suggest ways that cybersecurity can be a competitive advantage.

Many companies, including some large companies, ask their Chief Information Officer (CIO) to also take on the responsibility of CISO. I am not an advocate of this approach. The conflict of interest is obvious: many things that are very good for a strong cybersecurity program are not very good for a system administrator's ease-of-use to access your servers, or for a developer's ease-of-programming a new feature into an application. It would be much easier for an administrator to directly access any server from anywhere on the Internet rather than going through a Virtual Private Network (VPN), but doing so opens up a large security hole (see the story at the beginning of Question 11). If a developer did not have to check their code for common vulnerabilities that hackers exploit, they could possibly get more features into an application more quickly, but those features may lead to a security breach. It is helpful to visualize this issue in terms of building a car: if we took crash testing and vehicle safety off the table for automobile design, cars would be cheaper, lighter, more fuel efficient, and even perform better. The downside of doing this would be more serious injuries when accidents occur, and more automobile-related fatalities on the road. This is, of course, unacceptable, so crash testing and vehicle safety are critical design aspects of any car. Normally, a head of safety for any new automobile design works in a "healthy tension" between the people in charge of vehicle performance, vehicle fuel efficiency, and vehicle price. To put one person in charge of more than one of these areas creates an obvious conflict of interest. Similarly, if you put one person in charge of both your information technology as a whole and your cybersecurity program, that person will face the same conflict of interest.

Finally, it is critical that everyone in your company knows who is responsible for cybersecurity. Employees need to be trained on what issues to bring to this person's attention (or to the attention of the group that reports to this person), on how the company defines success when it comes to cybersecurity, and the role that they play to keep your company safe from cyber threats.

To summarize, your company needs a CISO, either an external part-time contractor or a full-time team member. This person should not report to your CIO (or be your CIO). This person needs to have a strong understanding of how your organization works operationally, not just technically. Your CISO needs support from you and your executive team in order to incorporate cybersecurity as part of your company's culture. Your team needs to know who the CISO is and how to make contact with this person if a cyber incident is suspected.

QUESTIONS TO EXPLORE this topic further with your company's leaders:

➤ Do we have a policy on who can proactively shut down systems based on a concern of cybersecurity risk?

➤ Who is the decision maker on if an incident is a cybersecurity issue?

➤ How do employees report concerns to the head of cybersecurity?

WHAT IS THE FIRST CALL I SHOULD MAKE IF MY TEAM SUSPECTS THAT A BREACH TOOK PLACE (OR IS TAKING PLACE)?

"We have only two modes—complacency and panic."

– JAMES R. SCHLESINGER, THE FIRST U.S. DEPT. OF ENERGY SECRETARY

MY CLIENT'S CFO, Jill, had a genuinely panicked tone in her voice, which isn't normal for her. She is one of those CFOs that has been doing her job for well over a decade and has seen pretty much everything before. She hadn't seen this. "Bryce, someone closed our payroll account. I can't pay my staff."

That got my attention. Saying "I can't pay my staff" is only one step away from saying "I'm out of business." This company was one of my first clients when I started my advisory services business, so I have a soft spot for them.

I tried to keep my tone as calm as possible, but she had me genuinely concerned. "Jill, who is 'someone'?"

"I have no idea. My staff just submitted a payroll run, and it was rejected. I called the company that does our payroll, and they claimed that I called them a week ago and cancelled our services. I never made that call."

"I believe you Jill. Ask them to reactivate your account. When I was in payroll, we could reactivate a company for up to a year after they cancelled. It only takes a few minutes."

"They won't do it. They said that as soon as an account is closed, it can't be re-opened. They want to start us as a new company with them, and it will take almost two weeks. Payroll is due in three days."

"How long have you been doing payroll with them?"

"Over five years."

"Perfect. That's what I wanted to hear. I know their CISO. Give me an hour and I'll call you."

"Bryce, I have to pay my staff."

"I know Jill, and you will. We can do a one-off payroll run manually if we need to, but tax calculations and vacation accruals will be a real challenge. Let's not rush to judgment. Give me an hour."

"What do I do in the meantime?"

"Call their customer service line and ask for Frank Lewis, their COO, by name. You will get his admin. Explain that you have been a customer for over five years and that someone fraudulently called them and closed your account. Tell them that they never authenticated whomever called them, and that you need their help to fix it. If that doesn't get you immediate attention, tell them that if you can't pay your staff on time, it will be a serious business disruption, and that determining who is at fault for that business disruption will be the purview of your respective legal departments. Lawyers are expensive, and it is not in anyone's best interest to go that direction. Getting payroll services resumed will be much less expensive for everyone involved."

There was a long pause on the phone. Jill was scared. Frankly, I was too. My client was in real trouble here, and I didn't understand why this would have happened. Who profits from this? What is the criminal angle to this? I tried to calm her as best I could. "Jill, please call them now. That company's CISO and I are good friends—I'm going to call him to see if they have had other instances of this type of issue, and you and I will regroup after that."

"Okay Bryce. What if they won't listen?"

"Let's worry about that when it happens. You will push their hot buttons, and it should get you the attention this issue needs." My mind immediately went to a cybersecurity breach. While I was pulling up the incident response plan that I had written for them the year prior, I asked Jill to look for anything else out of the ordinary. "Jill, I need you to focus on your other systems for a moment. Is anything or anyone else behaving strangely? Any issues reported by your team? Any odd behavior from your computers, from your ERP system, or from anything else?"

We had worked together for a long time, and she knew to take this question seriously. "Hang on Bryce." She put the phone down and I heard her walk out of her office. When she came back a few minutes later, I had their incident response plan in front of me. "No one is reporting any issues. Our ERP is fine. Email is fine. Internet connectivity is fine. Our remote users are VPN'ed in fine. It's just payroll."

"That's good news. Let's work the incident response plan. Please open tickets with your network services provider and your intrusion detection company and ask them to look for unusual behavior on the network. I'm going to call your payroll company's CISO. Let's regroup after we have more information."

I was able to get hold of him immediately. We had last seen each other in person just a few weeks earlier at a conference, but we have known each other for almost 10 years. "Chuck, someone called into your customer service department and impersonated my client. This person closed my client's account. How could someone monetize this? What angle is here other than business disruption?"

He paused for longer than I expected. "I haven't heard of this before, Bryce. Our biggest cyber issue is criminals filing fraudulent tax returns for our customers' employees. What day did the call come in to close the account?"

"October 31st. Halloween."

He thought for a moment longer. "I'm going with simple business disruption on this. The fact that it was Halloween makes me think someone had too much to drink and an axe to grind. Ask your client if anyone has left their payroll department recently who had their account number and knew that we did their payroll. I don't see a way for a criminal to profit from this. I'm guessing that someone wanted your client to go through exactly what they're going through."

Chuck was right. A quick review of the clients' intrusion-detection system turned up nothing. The evidence was not concrete—it never is when trying to prove a negative—but we had enough information to move ahead with a working theory that this was not a cybersecurity breach, but rather a procedural breach that allowed someone to impersonate my client's CFO and cause a significant business disruption. The most probable explanation is that a former employee wanted his or her old boss to have a very bad day, and had found a good way to accomplish this goal.

A likely suspect quickly emerged. A former employee of my client had left several months earlier on unfavorable terms, and while there was no proof of attribution, this person was a likely culprit. Because they were no longer an employee, there was very little that could be done at this point. My client added procedures to change the account numbers of their critical bank and payroll accounts whenever an employee left their finance team.

NOTE: Since that time, the payroll company has also added authentication questions for anyone calling in to close an account.

The story above makes an important point: Knowing whom to call when something is wrong (or suspected to be wrong) is just as important as the specific steps to follow after calling those people. In fact, often it is more important. Every cybersecurity incident is different. In the above example, it turned out not to be a cybersecurity incident at all. That isn't the point, though—in order to rule out a cybersecurity issue, a sweep of all cyber detection systems is required.

It is much easier *before* a cybersecurity incident occurs to document a list of specific people to call, rather than after the fact.

Calling in experts to determine possible motivating factors for the incident is important. The goal is to get a picture of what is going on as quickly as possible, and calling the right people is the best way to accomplish that goal. It is much easier *before* a cybersecurity incident occurs to document a list of specific people to call, rather than after the fact.

Here are some examples of who should be on your list:

1. Your cybersecurity team. These people may be outsourced or they may be in-house. Companies specialize in cybersecurity incident preparedness and detection, and having an existing relationship with them is extremely helpful.

2. Your CISO. While a CISO is normally not the person that would be hands-on for an issue like this, the story at the beginning of this chapter was picked for a reason—not all cybersecurity incidents have anything to do with traditional cybersecurity. A good CISO can help you determine the most plausible scenario for the situation you are facing. Don't have one? Consider retaining one, as you would retain legal counsel or accounting services.

3. Your cybersecurity insurance company. If you don't have cybersecurity insurance, I would strongly advise you to price out a policy. Many of these companies are designed to help you handle an incident, not just pay for the cost of an incident. They may have their own team of

cybersecurity remediators, legal counsel, and other groups that will quickly address your issue. A good cybersecurity advisor can help you find companies that provide this type of coverage.

4. Executive management. If any reasonable possibility exists that a serious cybersecurity incident (or business disruption) is taking place, your executive team needs to know. Their guidance can help coordinate efforts across departments, and can also be useful to put multiple pieces of information together to form a "big picture" of what is going on. Enough said.

5. Depending on the severity of the incident and the likely culprit(s) responsible, law enforcement can be a strong ally in incident response. Generally speaking, the Secret Service handles incidents involving credit card theft or fraud. The FBI handles fraud from wire transfers or general hacking/fraud that originates overseas. Note that the FBI will normally not get involved in incidents under $1 million, but that is not a hard-and-fast rule. It is important that the decision to engage law enforcement be done in concert with executive management and with your insurance company.

6. Your clients. If the incident you are having impacts your ability to service your customers, it is in your best interest to begin notifying them of the situation immediately. If the incident does not impact production, then customers should not be notified as part of a "first response" effort.

In the midst of a crisis, it is critical to have a playbook to respond to an incident. It needs to include who your key players will be during an incident, procedures to contact each person, and a description of the role each one of these people plays. Post-breach, you will likely be speaking with law enforcement, with regulators, with your clients, with attorneys, and with the media. **Your company will be assessed on the speed and quality of your response to the incident.**

> **QUESTIONS TO EXPLORE** this topic further with your company's leaders:
>
> ➤ Do we have a playbook on how we investigate suspected cybersecurity incidents?
>
> ➤ What is our communication and escalation process on suspected incidents?

WHAT DO MY EMPLOYEES NEED TO KNOW ABOUT CYBERSECURITY?

"People always make the best exploits. I've never found it hard to hack most people. If you listen to them, watch them, their vulnerabilities are like a neon sign screwed into their heads."

– ELLIOT ANDERSON (RAMI MALEK) FROM "MR. ROBOT"

MOST COMPANIES IN the manufacturing industry have a head of plant safety. This is a critical function, and OSHA demands that some very specific directives be followed in order to keep your plant floor a safe place for your employees to work. Some of those directives include proper training on how to use the machinery on the floor, and the incident response plan to follow when things go awry. I was a chemistry major for my undergrad work, and anyone in that field knows that fighting a sodium fire with water is going to result in a bad day for everyone involved. Fighting a wood or paper fire with water will usually work well, though. If you happen to have metallic sodium in your manufacturing plant, it's critical to train your employees on which extinguisher to grab, depending on the circumstances. Their life may depend on it.

Cybersecurity has similar rules. If you are not educating your employees on cybersecurity best practices, you are missing the biggest opportunity for improvement in your entire cybersecurity profile. Your employees have business-need access to a *lot* of important data, and their ability to protect that data—or to inadvertently let it walk out the door of your organization—is strong.

Lack of education was at the heart of a number of incidents of a major security breach. You have probably heard about the new HR employee that got an email from the president of the organization asking for all the W2 information on every employee, so that person sent them exactly as instructed. The employee did not recognize the fact that the email came from a hacker impersonating the CEO, and a major security breach took place.

A cybersecurity awareness culture is critical to the success of your company. Employees need to understand how their actions positively and negatively impact the cybersecurity posture of your company.

Entire business models are based on this kind of fraud. Let's pretend that I am going to build a site with the world's best collection of cute pet pictures. I'll give you the first 10 for free (and those 10 are the most adorable pictures you have ever seen), but to see more, you need to set up a username and password. The access is still free, though.

No big deal, right? Wrong. In this scenario, I own this website and I am a criminal, and my business model is to try to use the username and password you just entered at every major banking website, on all major email providers, on your company's VPN portal, and *anywhere else that I think you might have used the same username and password*. I will then extract any valuable information I can from those sites, sell the information for a profit, possibly ransom your own data from you to make even more money, and then move on to the next victim.

Question: Can you just institute a strong password policy and the problem of guessable passwords will go away? Think again. The password "abc@123" will pass Microsoft's strong password policy. So will "Pa$$worD." So will "Summer2019!" All of these are on a hacker's list of passwords to try. Your users need to understand how to build a password that is genuinely challenging to guess, and a cybersecurity training program will educate them on how to do that. See Question 16 section 1 for examples of how to create a good password.

The explosion of social media represents a new opportunity for your marketing, sales and customer service areas, but it poses a serious risk where employees can unintentionally cause irreparable damage. Facebook profiles that include a person's full birthday makes it easier for a cyber-criminal to impersonate that individual. LinkedIn profiles are a goldmine when it comes to finding key leaders in an organization. Hackers use these profiles to craft very convincing phishing emails that impersonate you and your leadership team. "Selfie" pics may have a whiteboard in the background with company secrets on it.

Your employees need to be educated on cybersecurity best practices.

Your employees need to be educated on cybersecurity best practices. Companies specialize in this type of training, and they may or may not be a good fit for your company culture. Picking the right type of training is critical; having a good cultural fit is more important than the actual content. Be sure to do proper due diligence to ensure that the training content offered by the company or companies you are considering is a good fit for the culture of your company.

The specific issues that I would recommend any cybersecurity awareness training program address are as follows:

1. How could a cybersecurity breach impact my company's ability to serve our customers, or even to stay in business (see Question 10)?

2. Why is it important to keep sensitive company data secure (see Question 2)?

3. How could information shared on social media lead to negative consequences for the company?

4. Why is it important that everyone uses strong passwords and does not share them (see Question 16, section 1)?

5. Why are administrator rights (full control) to my desktop or laptop a bad idea (see Question 16, section 5)?

6. What is phishing, and what are the clues to detect a phishing attempt?

7. If I fall for a phishing attempt, what do I do? Who do I call?

8. What tricks do cybercriminals use to try to fool me into helping them hack my company?

9. Why is it important that my PC, smartphone, and other devices perform periodic patches/updates?

10. Who is ultimately responsible for cybersecurity at my company (see Question 6)?

11. What cybersecurity regulatory issues does my industry/company adhere to, and what are the penalties if we do not (See Question 9)?

12. What role do I play in the overall cybersecurity plan of the company?

The important message here is that you already know you must train your employees on certain things in order to have them perform their job functions. Cybersecurity is one of those things. If you are uncertain as to how to structure a cybersecurity training program, find an advisor that can help you.

QUESTIONS TO EXPLORE this topic further with your company's leaders:

> ➤ When was the last time you were trained on cybersecurity? What did you take away from it?

> ➤ Do your team members who have access to sensitive data get additional training above and beyond those who do not?

WHAT STANDARDS OR REGULATIONS FOR CYBERSECURITY SHOULD MY COMPANY USE AS THE BASIS FOR A CYBERSECURITY PROGRAM? PCI? HIPAA? NIST? COBIT?

"In the very near future, cyber security exercises are going to be absolutely expected of all companies by regulators."
— MICHAEL VATIS, FOUNDING DIRECTOR OF THE FBI'S
NATIONAL INFRASTRUCTURE PROTECTION CENTER

HAVE YOU EVER tried a new diet or exercise regime? Have you ever switched from the Atkins diet to the Mediterranean diet to the Paleo diet? These variations on a theme have one thing in common: If you eat a little less and move a little more, you will probably lose weight. If you follow P90X or Spin Class or CrossFit, it will still boil down to the simple truth that moving your muscles and stretching your tendons/ joints will likely make you live longer, and will probably make you feel better at the same time.

The intricacies of specific cybersecurity frameworks should not be a concern of a non-technical business executive or owner. However, it is good to understand which framework applies to a particular situation. Let's break them down into two groups: frameworks and laws/directives:

Cybersecurity Frameworks:

NIST (National Institute of Standards and Technology): The NIST group has been working to bring standards to scientific areas for over 100 years. They have two distinct standards for cybersecurity: 1) NIST 800-53, which is a set of detailed security controls for federal information systems, and 2) a more general cybersecurity framework. For many organizations, the NIST framework is a very good place to begin a cybersecurity program. In 2017, a new executive order was signed which requires the heads of all US government agencies to "be guided by the NIST Framework for Improving Critical Infrastructure Cybersecurity."[35] NIST is completely free to use, and is offered up by the USA government in the hopes that it will serve the common good.

ISO 27000 (International Standards Organization):[36] The smart people at the ISO have come up with a set of frameworks for information security management, known as ISO 27000.[37] Its look and feel is similar to NIST, but NIST was developed with the USA in mind and ISO is more global in scope. If you are doing a lot of worldwide business, ISO 27000 may be a better choice than NIST, but to be honest, most of both frameworks are interchangeable.[38] ISO charges fees to use its publications, whereas NIST is free.

COBIT (Control Objectives for Information and Related Technology): COBIT has been around in one form or another since the mid 1990's. COBIT is broad. Very broad. Broad as in mouth-of-the-Mississippi-River broad. The latest version is COBIT 5, and it has (shockingly) 5 pillars:

1. Audit and Assurance

2. Risk Management

3. Information Security

4. Regulatory and Compliance

5. Governance of Enterprise IT

COBIT is the kind of framework that is used to implement other frameworks across an organization. It contains several articles on how to implement NIST 800-53 (see above) using the COBIT model. For larger organizations, COBIT is a great way to have "one ring to rule them all" when it comes to your regulatory, cybersecurity, compliance and governance systems.

Cybersecurity Laws/Directives:

PCI (Payment Card Industry): Do you take credit cards? Well, the five major credit card brands have come up with an exhaustingly descriptive set of cybersecurity standards that you are supposed to comply with if you accept credit cards. To be honest, most of PCI makes a lot of sense. Not a bad choice on which to base a cybersecurity program. If you take credit cards and are not PCI compliant, you could be fined by the PCI board, or even be banned altogether from accepting credit cards.

PCI is not a law. It is a directive from those that offer and process credit cards.

HIPAA (Health Insurance Portability and Accountability Act): HIPAA was designed to ensure that individuals would be able to maintain health insurance coverage between jobs, and it also set standards to ensure the security and confidentiality of patient information.[39]

HIPAA has 18 separate "identifiers" that are considered Protected Health Information (PHI):

1. Names

2. Address (including zip code)

3. Dates (birth, admission, discharge, death)

4. Telephone numbers

5. Fax numbers

6. E-mail addresses

7. Social security numbers

8. Medical record numbers

9. Health plan beneficiary numbers

10. Account numbers

11. Certificate/License numbers

12. Vehicle identifiers and serial numbers (including license plate)

13. Device identifiers and serial numbers

14. Web Universal Resource Locators (URLs)

15. Internet Protocol (IP) addresses

16. Biometric identifiers, including finger and voice prints

17. Full-face photographic images and any comparable images, and

18. Any other unique identifying number, characteristic, or code

HIPAA is a very subjective standard relative to others. For example, HIPAA requires that, "reasonable precautions should be used to avoid sharing patient information with those not involved in the patient's care," but the definition of "reasonable" is left as an exercise to the reader. Over time many of the requirements have become easier to interpret, often as the result of litigation.

HIPAA is not just a set of guidelines. It is an Act of Congress. Compliance is mandatory. HIPAA has teeth: Civil penalties range from $100–$50,000 per incident and up to $1.5 million per year. Criminal penalties range from

$50,000–$250,000 and 1–10 years in jail. People have done serious jail time over HIPAA violations.[40]

DFARS (Defense Federal Acquisition Regulation Supplement): Do you do any work with the United States Department of Defense? If so, you should already know about DFARS.[41] What you may not know is that there is a section specifically addressing cybersecurity and rules around disclosing data breaches.[42] If you are in this industry or are considering joining this industry, I recommend going to the citations section of this book and reading up on these rules.

GDPR (General Data Protection Regulation): Do you do business within any European Union (EU) countries? Do you have any data at all on citizens of a EU country? If so, GDPR is a big deal.[43] GDPR focuses on protecting data *and controlling how you can use it* for anyone in the EU. You must get consent before collecting personal data. You must appoint a Data Privacy Officer for your company. You must do Privacy Impact Assessments. You must notify a "data protection authority" of a data breach within three days of discovering it. GDPR gives people the right to be forgotten, meaning that upon request, you must be able to purge your data of any trace of an EU citizen.

NOTE: GDPR has a different twist than the other regulations in this section. It focuses on privacy protection, and as such it has requirements that go beyond "traditional" cybersecurity concerns. Penalties for violating GDPR vary widely on the size/scope of the penalty, but worst case, it's 20 million Euros or 4% of a company's global annual turnover, whichever is greater. Ouch!

Which one of the above cybersecurity frameworks is best for you? There isn't an easy answer, and often multiple frameworks will impact your core business. As an example, many universities have a health clinic on campus, and its technology systems must comply to HIPAA. If the campus bookstore or cafeteria takes credit cards, those systems must comply with PCI. The campus admissions department must comply with

GDPR if EU students ever apply to the university. **The core takeaway is that you may have no choice but to comply with some requirements, and you may have the option to utilize others as tools on which to base your cybersecurity program.** This is a complicated decision. The best framework(s) for you depend on your industry, your geography, your size, the type of data you use to run your business, and any existing contracts you have with clients or future contracts you hope to win. It is important to pick a framework or frameworks that makes sense for your organization and to devise a plan to adopt those procedural and technical best practices. Answering this question for your specific situation is one of the things that a good cybersecurity advisor can help you accomplish.

Please see the Appendix for an expanded description of each of the above cybersecurity regulations/frameworks.

QUESTIONS TO EXPLORE this topic further with your company's leaders:

- ➤ What regulations is our company required to follow due to our industry?

- ➤ What regulations is our company required to follow due to our geography?

- ➤ What cybersecurity framework(s) do we find useful for our business?

- ➤ Where are we on implementation and practice maturity of the framework(s) we choose to follow?

HOW MUCH WOULD MY CUSTOMERS CARE ABOUT A CYBERSECURITY BREACH?

"The effect of a data breach can be devastating. When customers start taking their business elsewhere, that can be a real body blow."
– CHRISTOPHER GRAHAM, INFORMATION COMMISSIONER OF UNITED KINGDOM

I'M GOING TO lay my cards on the table. **It is true that the average customer response to a cybersecurity incident is typically more muted than many media sources would lead you to believe.** Having said that, customer response often involves them avoiding doing business with you if there are competitors available, especially in the first year after a breach. **If your business relies on trust from your customers as a primary motivator to do business with you, a breach will have much more serious consequences.** Let's dive into some specific examples of the impact of a breach, and then focus on customer response.

When I worked in the payroll industry, the stakes were high every day we went into the office. Friends used to tease me about being in such a "mundane" industry, but I saw it as anything but ordinary. Our product was important. Critically important. Employees were depending on receiving their paychecks. Employers were depending on my company to deliver accurate, timely payrolls every time, without exception. About 40% of employees live paycheck to paycheck. It isn't a pleasant statistic but it is a real one. If we assume that half of all employees have a child at home, 20 paychecks out of 100 were literally going to put food on the table for a child the next day. This level of pressure drove me to achieve. I loved it.

If your business relies on trust from your customers as a primary motivator to do business with you, a breach will have much more serious consequences.

In the end, we didn't sell the service of producing paychecks—*we sold trust*. We sold the outsourcing of a critical business process in order to allow our client to focus on the things that their company did that truly differentiated them from their competition.

A serious cybersecurity incident could have been the end of the company. We were one of the ultimate targets for hackers: we had mountains of confidential data on the employees of our clients, and we had a money transfer system that automated the movement of millions of dollars every day. In short, we were a very complex money-transfer service. If the bad guys got in, customer trust in our company would have eroded very quickly, and without trust, we had nothing to sell.

A company can be harmed in six primary ways:

1. *Breach remediation cost:*

   - Costs from companies that specialize in cybersecurity remediation.

   - Attorney's fees.

   - Public relations and possibly advertising fees.

- Increased fees to communicate with customers, vendors and government agencies about the breach.

- Increased insurance premiums going forward post-breach.

2. *Brand reputation damage/loss of customer trust.* Fewer new customers. Reduced sales to existing customers.

3. *Litigation liability.* Class-action lawsuits. Lawsuits from vendors and/or customers that experienced damages as a result of the breach.

4. *Direct financial penalties.* Fines from government regulatory bodies. Fines from private consortiums (PCI for example)

5. *Productivity losses due to systems being shut down or replaced on a timeline so short that it causes major disruption.* Productivity loss due to cuts in operational areas to compensate for an unplanned increase in spending on cybersecurity.

6. *Partial or total loss of parts of your business.* Losing the ability to take credit cards as a payment form, for example.

Let's focus on where your customers fit into the above areas. They may:

- Stop doing business with you.

- Demand that you spend more on cybersecurity without allowing for an increase in the price you charge them.

- Engage in civil lawsuits against you.

- Post nasty things about you in social media, which contributes to damage to your reputation.

In the end, the industry you are in, and your response to the breach, will both determine a great deal about how much your customers care about a breach. Let's look at some examples:

- **Neiman Marcus.** High-end retailer. 350,000 credit card records stolen.[44] *$1.6 million judgment in a class-action lawsuit,* of which only $400,000 is directed toward consumers.[45] Given the large number of records stolen, it's surprising that there was not a larger impact. *Total cost: hard to estimate, but the store is facing financial woes so severe that its future is in jeopardy.*[46]

- **Home Depot.** Largest breach in retail history. 56 million credit card records stolen. Direct costs totaling $62 million.[47] A $19.5 million settlement for class action lawsuits.[48] Some estimates point to the all-in total cost reaching *$10 billion* by 2020,[49] although to be honest that feels inflated to me.

- **Anthem breach.** Largest breach of healthcare data in history. 78.8 million records copied, likely by a foreign government. Real costs topping $260 million on security related measures alone[7], and another $115 million to settle lawsuits.[50] While Anthem was able to weather this storm, it is interesting to note that Anthem is one of the 11 major contributors to the HITRUST security framework.[51] Even those that help define cybersecurity best practices can still be victims. *Total cost: $375 million.*

- **Jeep** recall due to stunt hacking: In an attempt to shine a spotlight on vehicles that are potentially vulnerable to remote hacking, researchers found flaws in the specific way that Chrysler secured the Wi-Fi system of their 2014 model year cars.[52] Basic password security relies on using passwords that are essentially impossible to guess. Chrysler *meant* to re-randomize their Wi-Fi password every time a vehicle was started up by using a "seed" number based on the amount of time that had gone by since the vehicle was originally made, and (arguably) that's reasonably random. Instead, Chrysler made a mistake: they randomized the password BEFORE the car's computer received the current date and time, so each Chrysler car was using the same "default" timestamp of 12:00AM on January 1, 2013. The only difference between cars was the amount of time that passed between when the car was started and when the computer generated the Wi-Fi password, and those differences were only a few seconds depending on the model of car. The researchers then went a step further and were able to hack into Sprint's cell network system, where all Chrysler vehicles are connected.[53]

In 2016, they claimed to figure out how to rewrite the software that the car uses—and do much scarier things, such as disable the brakes or take control of steering.[54] Having said all of that, performing this hack requires that the hacker is in very close proximity to the car in question. It's never been done as an actual hack by people who mean to do harm. It simply isn't easy to do, but that didn't stop Chrysler from recalling 1.4 million cars due to the firestorm that erupted after the hack was disclosed. That also didn't stop a class action lawsuit from being filed.[55] *Total cost: unknown, but the expense of recalling 1.4 million cars, fighting a class action lawsuit and general reputational damage all adds up to a big number.*

- **Sony #1 (PlayStation): 2011.** Sony has been in the headlines too many times in recent years due to serious hacking issues. In 2011, their PlayStation network was hacked,

possibly exposing all 77 million users' personal information and 12.3 million credit card numbers. Sony had to shut
down their PlayStation network for a whopping 23 days as
a result.[56] Making money is hard to do when you are forced
to shut down an income stream for over 3 weeks. *Total cost:*
$170 million according to Sony's own estimate.[57]

- **Sony #2 (Sony Pictures): 2014.** Making movies about assas-
sinating leaders of foreign nations tends to really irritate
those leaders. A very nasty hack ensued, which exposed
everything from the movie in question to embarrassing
emails from Sony execs about some of the movie stars they
use in their movies.[17] *Total cost: Sony estimated $35 mil-
lion.*[58] *Others estimated as high as $100 million.*[59]

- **Code Spaces.** You may not have heard of this company.
They specialized in online services to allow programmers
to collaborate around the world. All programmers could
store their "source code" in the Code Spaces cloud service,
and Code Spaces had a 7-year track record of providing a
strong product for their customers. Code Spaces made the
mistake of storing their production servers and their
backups in the same cloud service. When their administration console was hacked, the hackers demanded that Code
Spaces pay a ransom or the hackers would delete their data.
When they refused, the hackers made good on their
promise. The irretrievable loss of data, combined with
brand reputational damage was unrecoverable.[60] The
posting on their website said it best: "Code Spaces will not
be able to operate beyond this point, the cost of resolving
this issue to date and the expected cost of refunding customers who have been left without the service they paid for
will put Code Spaces in an irreversible position both

financially and in terms of ongoing credibility." Twelve hours after the hackers got in, Code Spaces was out of business, never to return.[61] *Total cost: Bankruptcy. Out of business. Doors closed.*

What are the themes here? If your ability to service customers is compromised by hackers, your customers will care a great deal. If you are in a business where your reputation is based on trust or security, a breach will impact your bottom line, and may impact your ability to stay in business. Now that hacking often deliberately tries to prevent you from providing the product or service your company provides—which is the whole point of ransomware—your customers will likely care more about a cybersecurity incident than they would if the only cyber issue was a loss of privacy. Finally, lawyers are going to dream about huge dollar signs with the words "class action lawsuit" written below them. Lawsuits are expensive. Avoiding them is generally a good idea.

> **If you are in a business where your reputation is based on trust or security, a breach will impact your bottom line, and may impact your ability to stay in business.**

QUESTIONS TO EXPLORE this topic further with your company's leaders:

> ➤ How important is customer trust to our brand?

> ➤ Do our competitors try to differentiate themselves based on trust?

> ➤ What is it that we must protect to maintain our customers' trust?

WHAT IS MY PLAYBOOK IF I HAVE A CYBERSECURITY INCIDENT?

"Companies should be thinking about the legal and managerial decisions that the CEO, the COO and the board will need to make in that kind of crisis situation."

— MICHAEL VATIS, FOUNDING DIRECTOR OF THE FBI's
NATIONAL INFRASTRUCTURE PROTECTION CENTER

"I HAVE BEEN INVESTIGATING a large number of failed logins on the Microsoft Hyper-V server. The accounts that were attempting to log in were our managed service provider Service Admin Account and your Domain Admin account. Due to the volume of failed attempts, it does appear that the attempts are coming from an outside source. My company recommends that you reach out to a Security Firm to have your network investigated for a possible breach. Please let me know if you would like a recommendation."

I couldn't believe what I was reading. A new client I had started working with only weeks earlier forwarded me the email above from their computer network management provider. The owner of the business was concerned, and he had good reason to be. This was a healthcare company, and HIPAA breaches are serious. I had come onboard as their part-time CISO the month before, and the vendor that manages their network had kicked this ball squarely into my court. I had to figure out what to do and fast.

My priorities were simple:

1. Alert my client's executive team about the situation.

2. Determine if this is or is not a real hacking attempt.

3. If it is a real hacking attempt, determine how it is occurring.

4. Assess if the hack was successful in any way. Was any damage done? Was any data accessed?

5. If the hack was unsuccessful, terminate the hacker's access immediately.

6. If the hack was successful, start making calls to my client's CEO, their cybersecurity insurance carrier, a third-party company that specializes in breach remediation, and my client's attorney.

7. Follow-up with root-cause analysis and recommend preventive measures.

After calling the business owners and the company's CEO to let them know of the issue, I began working with their technology team to review thousands of failed login attempts. Over 500 per minute were being processed, and it was obvious that a classic dictionary password-cracking attempt was underway. I breathed a tiny sigh of relief to see that it had only started several hours earlier and appeared to be moving ahead at full steam, which meant that the bad guys had most likely not yet been successful at cracking an administrator-level password.

Now to figure out where it was coming from. The internal network showed no signs of trouble, and no unusual logins were found on the Virtual Private Network (VPN) portal. That left an Internet-based intruder as the only option. As soon as we put the pieces together, it was obvious what had gone wrong. A firewall configuration change from the night before had accidentally opened up several holes (called ports) from the Internet to an internal server (mistake #1). One of those ports, number 3389, was a common port used to remotely control servers (mistake #2). The server in question had not been configured to use a non-standard port for that remote-control functionality (mistake #3). Hackers worldwide that are scanning the Internet for computers that respond on port 3389 because they are an easy target.

This client didn't have a playbook on what to do when a cybersecurity incident is suspected, so we had to make it up as we went.

I had the offending ports in the firewall closed immediately. The login attempts stopped.

My blood pressure began to return to a more reasonable level.

The example above is real, and while it represents the best possible outcome of a cybersecurity incident, I used it here to make a number of points. This client didn't have a playbook on what to do when a cybersecurity incident is suspected, so we had to make it up as we went.

Doing so took extra time and might have led us to miss obvious steps.

- The executive management team did not have documented steps to take in their various departments to help bring operations back online if the hack had been successful, nor did they have procedures to follow if it was determined that any HIPAA protected data had been compromised.

- Their IT services vendor wasn't well trained in how to help us get to the bottom of the technical issues quickly, which lengthened the incident by hours.

- The client didn't have a checklist of whom to call when as a cybersecurity incident unfolded, which made my phone number the only number they thought to use.

What if I was unavailable when this took place? From a system design standpoint, I was a "single point of failure"—that is, if I wasn't available, the incident response process broke down. Not good. In a nutshell, we didn't yet have our act together, and it showed.

After an incident occurs, your company will be judged on the following criteria:

1. Did your company take all actions to prevent the incident that one would expect of a prudent organization?

2. Did your company respond to the incident using procedures that one would expect of a prudent organization?

3. Are there any ways that the media can portray your actions around steps 1 and 2 to make your company appear to be culpable or incompetent? If true, expect that they will. It attracts more readers to their publication.

A robust playbook that includes the involvement and actions of the President & CEO, Chief Legal Counsel, Chief Operating Officer, VP of Sales, VP of Human Resources, VP of Communications, Chief Security Officer, and the CIO and CISO will do immeasurable good in your ability to respond to an incident.

An incident response playbook needs several key elements to be effective. It must:

- Identify who in your organization has the authority to declare a cybersecurity incident. Who can initiate the playbook?

- Spell out how much money that person can authorize to be spent to have an incident investigated or remediated. If the CFO and CEO are out of town, this person needs to understand the parameters he/she can work within until the CFO or CEO can be reached.

- Have a list of the types of scenarios that it is designed to cover. Examples include the loss of sensitive data, a ransomware attack, the loss of a critical system, natural disasters, law enforcement contacting your organization about a warrant or subpoena, law enforcement contacting your organization about a suspected cybersecurity incident that you are unaware of, the loss of the use of one or more of your sites due to a natural disaster or because of other issues (such as a crime taking place in the building and the police barring your employees from entering the premises).

- Have a call tree that includes which people or groups to call when an incident takes place. See Question 7 for more on this point.

- Define the parameters under which law enforcement should be involved in a suspected breach, and the people or groups responsible for making the decision on when to bring in law enforcement.

- Include who can speak to the media about a cybersecurity incident, and what those who are not authorized to speak to the media should say if they are approached by a reporter.

- List all of your critical systems, the location of the data in those critical systems, and the location of the backups of the data for those systems.

- Have the maximum allowable downtime of each of your systems. This is called an RTO, or Recovery Time Objective. While it would be great if every system was always 100% up and running, that isn't realistic. Your mission-critical ERP system is usually much more important to your business than the computer monitors that display promotional videos in your lobby, for example. A realistic RTO for your ERP system may be 4 hours or even less. For those displays in the lobby, an RTO of a week or more may be acceptable.

- Have lists of the age of backup data for each system. You need a maximum amount of acceptable data loss per system, and your backup methodology for each system should be chosen based on that maximum, called an RPO, or Recovery Point Objective. Much like the RTO, it would be fantastic if every backup system had up-to-the-minute copies of your data, but for most of us, that is prohibitively expensive. Typically, three schools of thought exist about RPO's:

    1. You may have a regulatory or contractual obligation that spells out your RPO. In that situation, it's a moot point for you to come up with your own.

    2. You may be a large enough organization so that it is worthwhile to go through each system and have a discussion on the impact of losing one hour's worth of data, 2 hour's data, 4 hour's data, and one entire business day. Then get rough costs on backup solutions

for each RPO. Make your business decision for each system by taking those data points into account.

3. Make your RPO one business day for everything, run nightly backups on everything, and move on with life.
The best answer on RPOs for your organization depends on your situation.

- Cover the general incident-response process. While every scenario is different, this process normally follows these steps: preparation, detection/analysis, containment, eradication, recovery, incident closure/root-cause analysis, and preventative measures.

- Be reviewed on a frequent basis. These plans get stale quickly, and need to be reviewed whenever a significant change in your organization takes place.

If the above points are reviewed as a group, an interesting trend emerges. *Most of them are non-technical.* The majority are operational and financial in nature. That is a critical misstep in many incident response plans. If your technology team manages your incident response plan, they are making business and financial decisions that should be made by CEOs and COOs and CFOs and legal counsel. Your technology team should be advising a non-technology executive—often the COO or CEO—on any technology issues that directly impact the plan, but a non-technical executive should own it.

Your incident response plan needs to be tested. This is too important to be left to guesses.

Above all, your incident response plan needs to be tested. Unless you have tried out an incident response procedure, you're only able to guess if it will work. This is too important to be left to guesses. Question 12 deals with incident response plans in more detail, but it's worth repeating here.

The companies I have worked with that get their playbooks right have a distinct difference from those that do not: playbooks that are used often are much more useful than those that are rarely touched. While this is easier for larger companies to accomplish than smaller ones, it is often the smaller companies that are more in need of an up to date incident response plan when issues arise.

The takeaway messages from this section are easy to list:

- Your company needs an incident response playbook.

- The incident response playbook should be owned by a non-technical member of your executive team. Most decisions in the playbook are operational, financial or communications specific, not technology specific. Technology leadership should play a supporting role, not a primary role.

- Your company needs to periodically test your incident response capabilities.

- Your company needs to update the playbook from lessons learned as a result of tests, whenever significant changes occur to the operational or technical aspects of the company, or when merger/acquisition activity occurs.

QUESTIONS TO EXPLORE this topic further with your company's leaders:

> How do we test our incident response playbook?

> How often do we test it?

> What did we learn from our last test?

HOW DO I KNOW IF MY INCIDENT-RESPONSE PLAN IS GOING TO WORK THE WAY IT SHOULD?

"There are risks and costs to a program of action—but they are far less than the long range cost of comfortable inaction."
– JOHN F. KENNEDY

THE WHOLE BUILDING shook briefly. I heard several abrupt shrieks outside of my office. My computer monitor continued to glow, but the overhead lights went out. I got out of my desk chair and interrupted the person on the other end of my phone call. "I have a potential life safety issue. Please do not call the authorities. I have to go." I hung up the phone and ran out of my office. "Is everyone okay?" When someone shouted my name, I turned to see several people pointing out the window. The tips of flames were visible through one of the outside windows, which didn't make any sense given that we were three stories off the ground. I walked toward the window, and then everything started to make sense. A power pole near the building was on fire. The large transformer on top of it had blown up, and one of the power lines normally connected to it was laying on the ground, occasionally arcing with an intense blue light. A grass fire was starting, but the grass was surrounded by sidewalks on every side, so the fire was unlikely to spread.

Someone on my team had already called 911, and the fire department was on the way. Two people from desktop support started walking the floor, looking for people who had not plugged their monitors into one of the outlets wired for battery power, and unplugging any fans, desk lights and other non-essential items. The generator kicked in about that time, and the overhead lights came back on for our floor. From the center vestibule, we could see the two floors below us, and neither had lights that we could see. People were staring up at us, wondering how we still had power. We had a dedicated diesel generator and 4,000 pounds of batteries to tide us over until the generator could get up to speed...that's how.

Four months earlier, we had simulated a power outage as part of our annual disaster recovery planning (or Business Continuity Planning in corporate speak). We found a few problems. Some of the computers in the check-printing room were not wired into the battery backup power circuit. The cooling system in our datacenter shut down during the test due to incorrect wiring. The bill for the electrician to fix those two issues was almost $10,000 and our CFO was quick to point out that was an unbudgeted expense. Today those fixes were keeping us in business.

The CEO found me as I was walking to the printing room to check on their status. "Where are we at?" he said quickly. I was already confident because of the test four months earlier. "Everything is up. We don't have building A/C when the power is out, so it's going to get hot in here. Ask the ops team to start down the call tree for second shift. Everyone is going to want to be in shorts and t-shirts today."

"How long can we run like this?"

"We have 9 days of diesel, and a tanker truck is available with 24 hours' notice. We're good."

Thankfully it took only three days for the power company to get service restored to the building. It was a long time to be without power, but we had planned for this and knew how to handle it. Other than dealing with the drone of box fans, catered lunch because the building cafeteria was without power, and the most relaxed dress code I had ever seen at a payroll company, things ran pretty much as they always did. Our customers got their paychecks on time. Our staff morale remained high. Our P&L for the month was unaffected, outside of a bill for diesel fuel. It was as close to flawless as an unexpected business interruption could get.

Incident-response planning consists of 4 steps:

1. Establish internal service level agreements (SLAs). How long can we be down without a serious business impact? What is meant by "down"? Which of our systems is most critical? Which can we live without, and for how long?

2. Devise methods to meet those SLAs. Determine the budget for those SLAs to become a reality and figure out where those funds stack up in the priority of your business needs. It may take redundant servers or even a redundant datacenter. It may take backup generators. It may take new contracts to be negotiated with your vendors so that your SLAs can be met.

3. Implement the new systems/procedures/redundancies to have your SLAs met.

4. Test your systems with real-world tests. On a slow day or over a weekend, physically shut off the primary servers for your critical systems and try to recover at your off-site location. Take the database server offline and see how long it takes to restore those critical files from your backups.

It sounds so simple, but in truth, it rarely is. Unexpected issues come up during these tests. Database files that you thought were being backed up are nowhere to be found. Redundant Internet connections that were purchased years ago are now woefully inadequate to handle your business load today. Your business is constantly changing and evolving. I have yet to do a disaster recovery test and not discover at least one significant gap. There's always a new gap. It's to be expected, and it isn't a bad thing. It is why we test!

Incident-response planning can go too far. Businesses that spend too much time planning for the worst are giving up opportunities to expand and innovate. Businesses that spend too little time planning are at risk of serious business disruption if things go sideways. Remember the Code Spaces story in Question 9. Your business is too important to let criminals bring it to a halt. Be sure to make an incident-response test that fits with your business and your risk tolerance. If you are unsure what makes sense, there are consultants that specialize in this type of work.

> **There's always a new gap. It's to be expected and it isn't a bad thing. It is why we test!**

While many news-making headlines on cybersecurity deal with data theft, cybersecurity incidents designed to cause business disruption, such as Petya/NotPetya,[62] are far more common.

- Ransomware is designed to lock up your data so that you can't do business.

- Denial-of-service attacks are designed to knock out your web or email servers.

- Data destroying viruses attempt to disrupt your business by deleting the data you need to run it.

- System destroying viruses (such as Petya/NotPetya) are designed to scramble entire hard drives, erasing all data and causing all functionality of a system to go offline.

- New Internet-of-Things viruses are designed to destroy
  the device they infect, such as the April 2017 "Brickerbot"
  attack.[63]

These sorts of attacks are where cybersecurity and disaster recovery intersect. Doing a good job at one strengthens the other.

Many companies have a disaster recovery plan, but an untested plan is often so full of gaps that it is useless in a real emergency. Testing in real-world scenarios is critical. "Table-top" exercises where people talk through an incident aren't completely worthless, but weak points will not be found without stressing your procedures and your systems. Want to test what happens when the power goes out? Flip the circuit breaker that provides power to your building and see what happens. It's the only way to know for sure.

Furthermore, if an incident is of an unknown origin, it is a good idea to assume a cybersecurity issue until proven otherwise. This is for two important reasons: 1) If it does turn out to be a true cybersecurity incident, you are already one step ahead. 2) If it isn't, you just had a chance to exercise your cybersecurity incident response plan in a real-world scenario. It's a win-win.

Many companies have a disaster recovery plan, but an untested plan is often so full of gaps that it is useless in a real emergency.

There are several different levels of testing for incident response planning, and the amount of effort and benefit to you varies widely between them:

1. Test restore, local: Run a test to restore a file from a local
   backup to your production system. If your production
   system is in the cloud, this may not be applicable.

2. Test restore, cloud: Assuming you have local production
   systems and a cloud-based offsite backup (and I highly recommend a cloud-based offsite backup), run a test to restore

a file from the cloud back to your production system. Note how much time it takes to recover a file, and then use that information to estimate how long it would take to pull an entire server from a cloud backup. Depending on the size of your Internet connection and the size of your server, this answer might be measured in days, not minutes or hours.

3. Test of alternative production systems, offline: If you are running critical systems locally at your site, you should consider having a redundant datacenter that you could use in an emergency. For example, if your building was to be damaged by fire or flood, or even if there are rolling power outages that will last longer than your backup power. This happened in large areas of Japan after the Fukushima nuclear disaster in 2011.[64] In our current cloud-based computing world, services like these are much less costly than you may imagine. There are services specifically designed to keep an asynchronous rolling copy of your data in an offsite datacenter, and that datacenter will have servers on standby for you to use in the event of an outage at your primary site. A disaster recovery expert can help you decide the best choice for your situation. If you subscribe to a service like the one described above, it is important to test it. Your service provider can "light up" copies of your servers in a test environment—which should not be exposed to the Internet or to your production systems—and your internal staff can test if those systems appear to be working as they should. Your production systems will remain functional for the entire test.

4. Test of alternative production systems, online but after hours: If you are a 24x7 operation, ignore this paragraph and skip to section 5. A terrific way to test a remote datacenter is to shut down your production datacenter and see if

your systems can operate out of your remote environment. This requires a much more complicated test than in #3. You need to do this when your customers are not depending on your systems being available. You need to shut down your production datacenter, have your service provider stand up emergency servers, and expose those servers to the Internet so that your team can do real-world testing. You also must find a way to keep your real customers from using these alternative servers so that no "real" data is written or "real" transactions are processed from the offsite system. When the test is complete, your service provider will remove the emergency servers, and finally you must turn your normal production servers back on. If it sounds somewhat complicated, that's because it is. It is also a very solid test that should give you reasonable confidence that you have emergency services available if you ever need them. There are a few gaps left, though, that are covered in the next section.

5. Test of alternate systems, during normal production hours. This is "the big test." Some early morning, before your business begins experiencing heavy loads, you will shut down production systems and have your service provider light up your offsite servers. You will expose them to the Internet and begin running your business from them, preferably for at least one full business day. Real transactions will take place. Real customers will be using these offsite systems, although if the test is going as it should, they will be unaware of it. You will be able to judge the responsiveness of these systems during actual production use. When the test is over, you then have to run the entire scenario in reverse to get back to your primary systems. That means backing up all data from the offsite system to your

local servers, taking the offsite systems offline, bringing your local systems online, and when services are restored, deleting the offsite servers. This is time consuming and complicated. It will also give you the only *guarantee* that your incident response plan is going to work as it should.

If your company is in an industry or is of a size where 24x7x365 uninterrupted uptime is imperative, then none of the above situations may apply to you. A more advanced scenario such as multiple datacenters that are simultaneously live and can load balance between them could be the best choice. In order to accomplish that, your application must be specially written so that it can coexist in multiple places at the same time, and different databases can update each other simultaneously. Large companies such as Ebay, Amazon and Google have custom-built applications that do a great job at this, but they also have development budgets larger than most companies' total annual revenue. Deciding if an undertaking of this size makes sense for you depends on how expensive system downtime is and your overall risk tolerance.

Deciding if an undertaking of this size makes sense for you depends on how expensive system downtime is and your overall risk tolerance.

While Question 12 is a bit on the technical side, it covers this level of detail so that you as a business owner or executive can understand why a certain budget is required to do a specific level of testing. Incident response planning is still largely a non-technical exercise, per the examples given in Question 11.

For a business owner or executive, the key takeaways from this question are as follows:

1. If you have not done a live test of your disaster-recovery scenarios, you have no idea how effective they will be when you need them. Many F100 companies have not taken their

incident testing all the way to step 5, and there are many stories where not doing so has cost them during times of crisis. How far you need to take your testing is up to you and your trusted advisors.

2. If you do not make the budget available for real-world testing to be done, your technology teams will be unable to provide adequate support when an actual incident occurs.

3. If incident response plans are not used frequently, your team will not be as familiar with them as they need to be to use them effectively when the stress and confusion of a real incident is complicating matters.

It is up to you to make incident response planning and testing one of the priorities for your company. If you set the example, others will take your lead.

QUESTIONS TO EXPLORE this topic further with your company's leaders:

➤ How does our company assess the success or failure of an incident response test?

➤ When was the last time a test was done and what were the findings?

➤ Which systems would shut down our business if we lost them?

➤ Has our incident response plan even been run by someone outside of the technology team to ensure that the leader in this department isn't the only person that can execute it?

WHAT ARE ALL THESE "NEXT-GENERATION FIREWALLS," "INTRUSION PREVENTION SYSTEMS," AND "SECURITY AS A SERVICE" SYSTEMS THAT PEOPLE ARE TRYING TO SELL MY COMPANY?

"As we've come to realize, the idea that security starts and ends with the purchase of a pre-packaged firewall is simply misguided."

– ART WITTMANN, VP, TECHNOLOGY, MEDIA AND TELECOM AT INFORMA

WE HAD BEEN lost for almost an hour at this point. Northern Wisconsin has a custom of naming roads with letters like "C" or "JJ," but different counties reuse the same names again and again, so the road names are meaningless unless you know which county you are in. We didn't. My dad and I were looking for our friend's cabin, and all we had to go on was a state map and a compass mounted on the car's dashboard. The compass was one of those old oil-filled compasses from the '70s that had spent too many years being baked in the sun. Some of the oil had leaked out, so the compass indicator stuck sometimes, breaking free to give a new reading only when the perfect bump on the road came along. Sometimes you could trust the compass…and sometimes it would lie to you. It was almost noon, so the sun was in the south sky, but when it went behind the clouds it became useless to help us find our way. Eventually my dad turned to me and said, "You know what's worse than being lost and having no compass? Being lost with a compass that you can't trust," and he ripped the compass off the dash and threw it out the window. We drove on, eventually finding an attendant at a gas station who could give us directions.

Many of today's intrusion-prevention systems are only a small step above that compass. Sometimes they give genuinely useful information, and at other times they give false positives for normal network activity, and fail to alert on the activity of a hack in progress. Breach detection relies on understanding the "baseline" of behavior in your network, and then looking for unusual behavior. It's not a black-and-white detection, and much like an unreliable compass, the person using it needs to understand areas where it is strong and where it has blind spots, otherwise it can lead you in the wrong direction. Detecting a cybersecurity breach (or attempted breach) is not an easy thing to do, because the bad guys are deliberately trying to evade detection.

I'm devoting one of the 20 questions in this book to this topic for a simple reason: these tools are the best we have today. They are getting better all the time, and when used in proper combination, they offer a genuine improvement in the level of protection that your company will have against cyber threats.

Because this area of technology is evolving at a rapid rate, I'm not going to give opinions on specific solutions. However, some constants are worthy of discussion.

There are two primary types of advanced "hacker detection systems": 1) Those that ignore the actual data on your network and focus on metadata instead (let's call these metadata-only systems), and 2) those that investigate the actual data being sent to and from—as well as within—your network (let's call these deep-packet inspection systems).

What is metadata, you ask? Good question. Metadata is data about your data. Pretend that you are in charge of the mailroom at your place of business. You are not allowed to open any envelopes to see what is inside. In this analogy, the information *inside* the envelopes is "data." The information on the *outside* of the envelopes is "metadata." Just by looking at the outside of the envelopes, you can usually tell who sent the letter, when it was sent, and you could also keep track of how often someone mails your company and how often someone at your company responds. This is how metadata is useful to detect security issues. If it is unusual for a certain computer to send thousands of pieces of information to a source outside of your company, then a lot of good information can be gleamed from metadata. Systems that rely on metadata only are usually less expensive and have a smaller impact on the performance of your network. One of the best services that these types of systems provide is to block computers on your network from visiting any servers or websites on the Internet that are known to be malicious. The companies that sell metadata-only systems maintain a constantly changing list of Internet computers that are up to no good. They will keep your users from being exposed to those malicious machines, which is a very good dose of prevention. Some of these systems have dropped in price to the point that they are surprisingly affordable, even for small offices or home offices.

However, metadata-only systems have blind spots. It's relatively easy for an advanced hacker to hide their behavior from them. Let's say that a hacker wants to steal your trade secrets. If they can divide the data they steal into small segments and send individual segments to different external servers, then your metadata-only intrusion detection system has less chance to pick up on their activity. This was part of the methodology that was used in the USA's Office of Personnel Management (OPM) breach mentioned in question 2, where the bad guys "chopped up [data] files to avoid causing suspicious traffic spikes."[12] If a hacker has breached an external system that your company often uses, then any data sent to that system will probably be ignored by a metadata-only system, even if it is data you would consider top secret.

Now let's move on to deep-packet inspection systems. A "packet" is a small piece of data that is transmitted across a computer network. Thus, a "deep-packet inspection" system looks through every bit and byte that enters, exits and traverses through your network. They are the ultimate gatekeepers of information, and as such they can "see" normal behavior at a much deeper level than their metadata-only brethren. This knowledge comes at a price, though. These systems are more expensive, more difficult to install and maintain, and they slow down the overall performance of your network.

Deep-packet inspection systems have an ace in the hole that cannot be ignored, and an Achilles heel that must be considered. Their ace in the hole is this: In order for these systems to work, they need to work with unencrypted data or they must be able to decrypt the traffic on your network. They can't examine encrypted data (that is the whole point of encryption—it's gibberish without the decryption keys). Your firewall administrator will need to program deep-packet inspection firewalls with every encryption certificate for every system you use, which means it's possible to set up these systems so that any data they can't decrypt is automatically blocked. This will make it much more difficult for hackers to hide an exfiltration of data.

A deep-packet inspection system has a downside. By definition, they have "the keys to the kingdom" when it comes to your encryption keys (also called certificates). While these systems tend to be locked down like Fort Knox, attacks are not unheard of even on highly locked down systems (such as the hack of the company RSA in 2011).[65]

Internet connection providers such as Verizon and AT&T are now offering external cybersecurity services that attempt to detect and prevent external hacks from occurring before the cybercriminals ever reach your systems. They also provide Security Operations Center (SOC) services that are staffed 24x7 with people ready to respond to any sign of a breach or attempted breach. These services offer a strong level of protection, but if you choose to use one, you need to have top talent on your end to manage them. Your own advisor needs to provide your external vendor a view of your priorities, and to act as your trusted advisor during cyber incidents. ALL companies offering a product or service look at their clients' needs through the lens of what their product or service can deliver. You need someone on your team that looks solely through the lens of what your company requires, not what a particular vendor has to sell you.

Your company should have one or more of these types of systems in place. The right one depends on your specific industry, your company size, and the type of data you need to protect. Often, a "defense in depth" approach where there are multiple separate layers of security makes terrific sense, if your budget allows for it and your external risks are large enough to warrant it.[66]

If you can't afford one of these systems yet, your systems administrator can do some basic things that will help detect bad behavior. A computer "honeypot" is a system designed to attract hackers or the malware they create (viruses, ransomware, etc.) in order to detect and terminate bad behavior. Here is one example: Make a folder on your file server called "accounting" or "payroll" or "topsecret" or something else that looks attractive to a hacker. Give all users rights to read and edit files in that folder. Add several dummy files in the folder with names such as "Q1Payroll.xlsx." Then add special features that will suspend any user account that tries to edit a file in that folder. A number of examples are available on how to do this that any competent IT person can follow.[67] Your administrator could also use a program to disable any account that writes a file with an extension of ".locked" or ".crypto" or ".zzz"

The two examples above are presented more for the idea behind them than the actual content. The key lesson from Question 13 is this: all of these approaches are based on detecting the *behavior* of a cybercriminal, not on a specific virus signature or a specific vulnerability in a particular operating system. Another term for behavior-based systems is Artificial Intelligence, or AI. You have probably heard about AI systems that can beat the best chess player in the world and can win at the TV game show "Jeopardy." AI is coming to cybersecurity. Quickly. The cybercriminals are already starting to use it, and if they have offensive weapons for which there is not a defense, we're in trouble. These AI-based systems are important for *everyone*, from a simple home office to a major government. They need to be part of your overall cybersecurity strategy.

QUESTIONS TO EXPLORE this topic further with your company's leaders:

> Do we have the right tools to detect cyberattacks?

> Do we have the right tools and vendor partners to react to a cyberattack?

> Do we have the right tools to protect against cyberattacks?

> Do we have trusted partners to help us make the best decisions on the tools above?

DO OUR VENDORS CARE IF THEY CAUSE A BREACH OF OUR DATA?

"If you think technology can solve your security problems, then you don't understand the problems and you don't understand the technology."

— BRUCE SCHNEIER, CRYPTOGRAPHY AND CYBERSECURITY EXPERT

I COULD FEEL MY face turning red, which is never a positive indicator that a phone conversation is going to end well. "Guys, we're transmitting passwords over the Internet in clear text. If this doesn't qualify as a 'red alert', what does?"

"Do you have any indication that you have been hacked?" the head of customer support for this vendor asked.

"Not yet."

"Someone would have to be listening in to get those usernames and passwords, and you're a small company."

I said, "We are a small *payroll* company. Your software is built for payroll companies. Outside of MoneyGram, how much more attractive a target *is* there to a hacker?"

"How much budget do you have available to fund the switch to SFTP?"

"Isn't it a business-as-usual function for you to keep your software secure? Your FTP system was built back in the days of modems, and it's 2002 now. Ninety percent of our clients are using the Internet to transmit their payroll data to us."

"We encrypt the data before sending it," he said.

"That is a big help, but it doesn't solve the username and password problem. The FTP authentication is being done in clear text. Any hacker worth his salt could use those credentials to get into our VPN and wreak havoc."

"Look," the man said, "I asked the development team to spec this out, and they are estimating $175,000 to re-engineer the software to use Secure FTP. If you have the funds for us to do it, let me know and I'll put it in the next available release. It isn't in our contract that we pay for user-requested enhancements. Users pay for user-requested enhancements."

I was beyond red-faced at this point because $175,000 was literally years' worth of licensing fees for this payroll software, and was also many months of profits for the payroll company I worked for. I could only imagine the look on the owner's face when I told him about this. I tried one last time to get the vendor to see reason.

"In the end I can't make you do this, but if we get hacked we'll possibly be out of business. That means we stop paying you your licensing fees. As soon as the hacker community finds out how easy it is to hack payroll companies that use your software, more of us will get hacked and go out of business. Then they will also stop paying you too. It's easy to get a list of the companies that use your software. We're all on your website. Please work with me on this."

"I can take you off our website customer list if you would like."

I figured it was smarter to hang up than to tell him what I was really thinking, and I also figured using as many four-letter words as I intended to use wouldn't be good for office morale. I told him thank you and hung up. I had a problem that genuinely threatened the company I worked for, the vendor didn't care, and I didn't have the money to make him care.

Rock meets hard place... I pulled the contract and read through it. He was right—the word security was mentioned only once, and it was about paying them a security deposit before they would install the software. Not helpful.

This example happened back in 2002, when only geeks, banks and the NSA really cared about cybersecurity. I fell into the first category, and the owner of the payroll software company apparently didn't. In the end, the story had a happy ending. I created a new domain just for that FTP server, stuck it in an isolated section of the network called a DMZ, and locked down the customer accounts one step down from Fort Knox. In 2004, I wrote up the idea for MCP

With only a few exceptions, a vendor is going to care as much about your cybersecurity as your contract with them forces them to care.

Magazine and had my first-ever published article.[68] I had to publish it under an assumed name, but it felt good when I used my grandfather's name, who had passed away in 1956 when my mother was a young girl.

Back to the present.

With only a few exceptions, a vendor is going to care as much about your cybersecurity as your contract with them forces them to care. Plain and simple. What are those few exceptions? If you are using a vendor that the media would rather report on than your company, and/or the vendor has more potential for reputational damage than you do, they may honestly care about keeping your company safe. Unless they are a household name and you aren't, this argument quickly falls apart.

Your contract is your best hope of having your vendors put some skin in the game. Healthcare companies are already familiar with this, because HIPAA requires a contract called a Business Associate Agreement (BAA). A BAA states that a vendor will follow HIPAA rules as it relates to your data. However, the vast majority of the BAA contracts I've read limit the liability of the vendor to the value of the contract they are signing with you. This is normally a pittance compared to the damage of a data breach.

The following is a list of ideas on how to ensure that your vendors are partners in your fight against cybercriminals:

- Require your vendors to submit to random audits of security practices associated with systems interfacing your company. It is best to have these performed by an independent third party rather than by you or by the vendor.

- Require your vendors to carry cybersecurity insurance that represents a minimum of 5% of your yearly revenue. If that is prohibitively expensive, it may make better sense to ensure that your cybersecurity liability policy covers the actions of third party vendors. Assuming that the vendor purchases insurance, require that your contract hold them liable for damages up to the limit of their cybersecurity insurance.

- Enforce a maximum time that vendors must install security patches into their production systems from third parties such as Microsoft or other software makers. A common goal is 30 days, although issues such as WannaCry are shortening this cycle.[1] [2]

- Require that vendors follow the same security regulations that you do, be it HIPAA, PCI, GDPR, or any other appropriate acronym. Just as important, add penalties for failure to implement standard cyber hygiene practices such as password management, log reviews, access control reviews, etc. One of the penalties must include that an incident found to be a negligent act of practice in cybersecurity is grounds for breach of contract and early termination without penalty.

- Let your vendors know that you will change to another vendor if they are unwilling to meet you halfway on cybersecurity concerns. It might be a good idea to change a vendor so that your other vendors know you are serious about this.

I don't want to be repetitive, but this one bears repeating: *A vendor is going to care as much about your cybersecurity as your contract with them forces them to care.*

DISCLAIMER: I am not a lawyer, nor have I played one on TV. Have a lawyer review your contracts.

QUESTIONS TO EXPLORE this topic further with your company's leaders:

> ➤ Do our contracts have language on cybersecurity?

> ➤ What penalties or liabilities do we ask from our vendors in our contracts?

> ➤ Which of our vendors have access to our sensitive data, and how do those vendor contracts differ from others?

WHAT IS ALL THIS "INTERNET OF THINGS" STUFF I HAVE BEEN HEARING ABOUT?

"I think computer viruses should count as life. I think it says something about human nature that the only form of life we have created so far is purely destructive. We've created life in our own image."

– STEPHEN HAWKING, THEORETICAL PHYSICIST

THE SUN WAS almost up, and I was tired. All-night working sessions were never my strong suit, but this couldn't wait. The plane would leave several hours later, whether my slide deck was complete or not. I had only two more slides to review for my upcoming presentation in Connecticut, and I needed a few good quotes to spice things up a bit. Internet searches are always a good place to start when looking for pithy quotes, but the Internet was not behaving itself. I kept hitting dead ends, and common websites were nowhere to be found. Nytimes.com was dead. Wsj.com was dead. Foxnews.com was dead. So much for any hope of finding some good quotes. Other parts of the Internet seemed okay, and my email was working, but given the early hour, I decided to get some sleep.

When I woke up around lunchtime, my inbox was lit up like a fireworks display. "Dyn DNS attacked." "Worst denial-of-service attack in history."

A distributed-denial-of-service (DDOS) attack occurs when thousands of computers begin flooding traffic to a specific point or points on the Internet, with the intent of making the target incapable of responding to legitimate requests. It's a way of bringing your system down without having to hack the system itself.

Wow! Sounds like the focus of my talk is about to shift. Digging into the articles revealed the truth: Threats about the power of a coordinated Internet-of-Things (IoT) attack just became real. Cybercriminals had already done this the month prior by attacking Brian Krebs's security website with IoT devices, but that was a single website. This attack impacted major sections of the Internet and disrupted businesses across the USA and overseas.[69]

Cybercriminals keep getting more creative in how they attack, and the IoT attack on October 21, 2016 is a good example of smart people doing bad things. Let's think like a terrorist for a moment. Imagine that you want to shut down all the roads in a large metropolitan area. You can try to do this a number of ways:

- You could bomb all the bridges from the air. While this was common during World War II, it requires that you have access to airplanes that can carry bombs, several pilots to fly the planes, and access to bombs, none of which is realistic.

- You could try to place explosives on the supports for all the bridges in the city and destroy the bridges that way, but that requires physical access to all the bridges and access to explosives, which would be very difficult.

- You could forget about the bridges, and instead steal thousands of cars and park those cars in the middle of all major intersections in the city. If you could manage to deploy all the cars at once, this approach could be very effective, but requires thousands of stolen cars and thousands of drivers who are all willing to walk home. Still difficult, and it's also temporary, because tow trucks will rectify this problem in under a day.

Now let's approach this from a cybersecurity standpoint: What if you could hack into the traffic light control system and turn them all green for 10 minutes. Imagine the number of car accidents that would take place. Imagine the blocked roads, the ambulances trying to respond to literally hundreds or thousands of accidents, the police trying to investigate all of these accident sites as crime scenes. It would be pandemonium and could take days to resolve. This would be an effective approach to accomplish your terrorist goal. Sometimes going after a control system is much easier and more practical than going after the system itself.

Sometimes going after a control system is much easier and more practical than going after the system itself.

The IoT attack that occurred on that day was a version of the scenario above. Computers don't like human-friendly website names, such as google.com or tcestrategy.com. Computers like Internet addresses that are effectively impossible for us mortals to remember, such as 216.58.216.238 or 107.180.27.156. To bridge the gap between people and computers, Domain Name Servers (DNS) manage an important feature of the Internet. DNS translates Internet addresses from user-friendly format to computer-friendly format. It is critical for websites, emails, and many other parts of the Internet to work correctly. The cybercriminals pointed over 100,000 IoT devices toward one of the largest providers of DNS services, Dyn, and flooded their servers with over one trillion bits of data per second. This is called a distributed-denial-of-service attack, or DDoS, and it was the largest such attack in history at the time.[70]

Many of the products we purchase today are not just a product. Twenty years ago, if you went into a store and bought a thermostat, you got exactly that: a thermostat. It controlled your heat and/or A/C, and had no ability to do anything else. It wasn't a concern beyond accurately running your heating or cooling system. Today, a thermostat is not just a thermostat. It's a computer that happens to be hooked up to temperature sensors and is programmed to control a furnace and air conditioner. Computers can be reprogrammed to do other things. Computers need to be protected from criminals that would try to make them do what the criminal wants rather than what you want. The Internet-connected thermostat, television, security camera, coffee maker, light bulb, juicer, refrigerator, washing machine, and other devices are now all computers. They all have the potential to be attacked, just like your desktop or laptop.

We have two inherent problems here: First, manufacturers are often not building reasonable security measures into these devices to keep them from being attacked.[71] Second, there are so many of these devices that, when used in concert, they can do genuinely harmful things. When 100,000 IoT devices ganged up on the Dyn DNS system, the IoT devices won. Imagine 100,000 angry bees attacking a single person. It's easy to figure out the winner in that fight.

Given the potential damage that these devices can do, the definition of an IoT device is important to understand. Differences of opinion exist on this, so I'm going to focus on the ones that meet the following criteria. For a device to be considered an IoT device, three conditions must be met. An IoT device must:

1. Have a computer as their "brain." By definition, almost anything with the ability to communicate with other computers is also a computer.

2. Be connected to the Internet. If you hook it up to a net-working cable or connect it to a Wi-Fi network, and that network can see external websites like Google.com, then this condition applies.

3. Be capable of receiving data. If a device can only send infor-mation and has been set up to be incapable of receiving it, then it cannot be remotely controlled.

Bluetooth devices do not fit the above criteria. Bluetooth cannot hook up directly to the Internet, and Bluetooth has a range of only 10–100 meters.[72] The limited range of Bluetooth cuts out 99.999% of all cyber-criminals around the world. This doesn't mean that there can't be vul-nerabilities with Bluetooth devices, because there most certainly are. However, a cybercriminal must have a much higher level of determination to get close enough to his/her target to interact with it. One caveat: many Bluetooth devices connect to a smartphone, and then the smartphone connects to the Internet. Whether the smartphone is the IoT device or the Bluetooth device is the IoT device is debatable, but if the informa-tion coming from the device goes over the Internet or if the device can be controlled from the Internet, then I would put it back in the IoT category.

Devices on air-gapped networks do not fit the criteria above. Most sub-F1000 companies do not have any air-gapped networks, though, so this rarely applies. (See section 9 of Question 16 for details on what an air-gapped network is.)

How can IoT devices be used against your organization?

1. As stated above, they can be used as an "infantry army" of devices to overwhelm other systems.

2. If your company is large enough to have many IoT devices internally, there are documented examples of these devices being used to slow a company's network to a crawl by a

hacker using them to send unwanted traffic throughout your network. A major university fell victim to this in 2016.[73]

3. They can be used as an entry point into your network. Without good network segmentation and good firewall rules, a hacked IoT device can be used as a means for a hacker to probe your network for vulnerabilities.

4. IoT devices may be giving away sensitive data, network passwords, or even your critical intellectual property without you knowing about it. Some of these devices are so poorly designed that they are broadcasting the "keys to your technology kingdom," such as your Wi-Fi password.[74]

5. The data your company is receiving from IoT devices can be manipulated if it isn't sent in a secure manner. This is a dark line of thinking, but with examples like Enron artificially creating power demand to drive up energy prices or VW cheating on diesel emissions, this risk is real.

   Imagine that your company owns farmland and uses soil sensors to determine the fertilizer needs of your land. Now imagine that a fertilizer company hacks into the sensor network and programs the sensors to report that fewer nutrients exist in the soil than are really there. You would buy more fertilizer than you need.

   Let's go even darker. What if a healthcare company starts offering IoT heart rate monitors to patients, and a company that sells heart medication hacks into the IoT network to manipulate the data in order to sell more of their medication?

Here's another scenario where the IoT could be used against more than just one company or one set of individuals. What if the IoT was manipulated against the public good? Here is an example of how this could play out. It's summertime. A large company has put in a bid for constructing a massive new power plant in a major metropolitan area. The debate on building the plant vs. increasing efforts to conserve energy is huge. Prominent people are on both sides. The vote to approve the project is in two weeks, and the weather forecast calls for some warm days ahead. On the warmest of those days, a hacker that has taken control of a few thousand IoT thermostats turns them all down 2 degrees. The hacker could even cause the displays on those devices to *not* display that the temperature has decreased, making the hack even harder to detect. An artificial brownout is created, which tips the scales on the city council vote to approve the power plant.

The hack could also be done by a group against the power plant. Wouldn't it be a great means to turn public opinion if an extremist group did a hack such as this—and then blamed the company that bid on the power plant?

I'll leave it as an exercise for the reader to think of other real-world scenarios where manipulation of public opinion such as this has played out. What concerns me most about this scenario is that it was not my idea. It was told to me by a person who works for a company that designs power plants.

So what to do about all this? Ask good questions before implementing IoT devices. Many IoT devices have genuine business value. I was speaking with the CIO of a major salon chain recently who told me that smart thermostats are saving them a whopping 30% on their heating/cooling bills. Other IoT devices might already be in your network that have a complete lack of any real business value, not to mention a lack of cybersecurity patching capabilities, or any support at all from their manufacturer. Would you let a laptop into your environment that had no support from its manufacturer or from the company that made its operating system? Of course not. Don't let your pretty Internet-connected fish tank lead to a cybersecurity breach that makes national news, the way a North American casino did in mid-2017.[75] An IoT device is a computer, like any other. It needs a reasonable level of cybersecurity and a genuine business value or it shouldn't be in your environment.

An IoT device is a computer, like any other. It needs a reasonable level of cybersecurity and a genuine business value or it shouldn't be in your environment.

The USA government is also taking action on IoT. The "Internet of Things (IoT) Cybersecurity Improvement Act of 2017" is specifically designed to require that IoT devices, "are patchable, do not include hard-coded passwords that can't be changed, and are free of known security vulnerabilities, among other basic requirements."[76]

Here are some questions about IoT devices that will help you make the best decisions for your company:

- Does this device add genuine business value? If it doesn't, don't allow it into your environment.

- Does the device need to be an IoT device to add that value? Is an Internet-connected coffee maker going to make your company more efficient? Or your workers have better morale? I doubt the cost-benefit ratio is compelling.

- Does the device collect or transmit sensitive data? If it does, be extremely careful to have appropriate due diligence done before implementing such a device.

- How is this product updated? New vulnerabilities are found in computers every day. When vulnerabilities are found, there needs to be a way to fix them. Some IoT devices have the ability to update the software in them, and some do not. You want the ones that do. In fact, some manufacturers automatically push updates. While this may sound a little scary because a hacker may find a way to push malicious updates, generally speaking the reward of updating the software of a system to protect against newly discovered vulnerabilities is higher than the risk of a manufacturer's update mechanism being hacked. The most notable exception of an automatic update gone wrong is the Petya/NotPetya attack of 2017 where the Ukrainian tax payment software MeDoc was infected with a very destructive virus.[62] However, the list of attacks that were prevented because of automatic update patches is a mile long. Patches are good.

- Is this device part of a system that will have a business impact if it fails? Generally speaking, IoT devices are more complex than the non-IoT version of the same device. Smart thermostats are a perfect example. *Nest Thermostat* is a leader in this space, and in early 2016, they pushed an update to their devices that caused some of them to stop charging their internal batteries.[77] In theory, this shouldn't be a problem because the furnace that any thermostat is attached to supplies power to the thermostat. This is how thermostats and furnaces have worked for decades. Nest built their thermostat so that it would not function if the internal battery drained, and when this glitch showed up, people literally lost heat in their homes and offices. How expensive do you think it would have been for Nest to add a "failsafe" mode to their thermostats so that if the thermostat's battery failed—or some other failure occurred where its software could not function as it was supposed to—such that the thermostat turns on the heater below 65 degrees Fahrenheit and turns it off at 66 or above? It's not an ideal solution but it beats losing all heat in your office. It is critical to ask these questions about any IoT device that will be a part of an important control system before purchasing them.

- Is the IoT manufacturer of the device in question part of the Industrial Internet Consortium? A group was created by IoT manufacturers to develop and share good cybersecurity best practices around IoT devices.[78] If the device you are considering is made by a company that is part of the Industrial Internet Consortium, the likelihood that their devices have reasonable cybersecurity is much higher. Alternatively, is your IoT manufacturer following the Department of Homeland Security's "Strategic Principles for Securing the Internet of Things"?[79] [80] If they have documentation on how they incorporate those principles into their products, it's a very good sign that they are taking cybersecurity seriously. Finally, a group called the Z-Wave Alliance is certifying IoT products to adhere to a reasonable level of cybersecurity.[81] [82]

- What is the lifecycle of the product? Most computer operating systems are supported by the manufacturer for a certain period of time, and are then deemed "end of life." The problem with end-of-life computers is that when new vulnerabilities are found, the manufacturer no longer fixes them. Microsoft operating systems are the most well-known example of this. The WannaCry ransomware took advantage of vulnerabilities that were not patched in end-of-life operating systems—at the time, Windows XP and Windows Server 2003. The issue was so serious that Microsoft chose to create patches for those systems even though they had gone end-of-life years earlier. Your IoT devices will have a lifecycle, and when the manufacturer deems the product end-of-life, you may have a serious risk if you continue to use it. It is important to know what that date is before you purchase an IoT product.

The above questions are not meant to portray that the IoT is inherently bad. On the contrary, many IoT manufacturers can *favorably* answer the above questions. Many IoT devices add huge business value. If they make business sense for you, use them. The bottom line is that IoT devices are computers, not toasters, even when they look like toasters, and they make toast. They are still computers, and they are still hackable. Make sure that the Internet-connected toaster or security camera or thermostat or medical device really needs to be an IoT device to bring business value to your organization.

QUESTIONS TO EXPLORE this topic further with your company's leaders:

> ➤ What IoT devices exist within our company and why?

> ➤ How many total devices are attached to our networks?

> ➤ How do we know that the devices on our networks have a reasonable level of cybersecurity?

ARE THERE "BLOCKING-AND-TACKLING" THINGS THAT I SHOULD BE DOING AROUND CYBERSECURITY?

"Companies spend millions of dollars on fire-walls, encryption and secure access devices, and it's money wasted; none of these measures address the weakest link in the security chain."

– KEVIN MITNICK, HACKER

YES, THERE ARE several. After the OPM breach, the US Federal CIO at the time, Tony Scott, refocused the government on cyber-security "basic hygiene."[12] I met Tony back in 2009 when he was the CIO at Microsoft, and he had a similar down-to-earth thinking on technology. Much like good ideas around staying healthy (eat right, exercise, get a good night's sleep, etc.), cybersecurity has many best practices that are universally good ideas, are not complex or expensive, are easily understood by non-technical people, and don't take years to implement. While most of this book focuses on more general topics of cybersecurity, some of the basics are just too important to ignore. Let's run down the list:

1. **Implement real password policies.** There's no easy way to say this, so I'm just going to say it. Passwords suck. They are no fun to create, no fun to remember, and no fun to type in. Okay, enough with the negativity. Passwords are still the most common authentication method today. **It is imperative to implement a password policy requiring complex passwords that can't easily be guessed, and have end-user training to go along with it**. Microsoft's Active Directory "require complex passwords" setting is a start, but end-user training is also mandatory. As I mentioned in Question 8, Pa$$worD will pass as a complex password, but it's also on every hacker's list of password dictionary attacks. I first heard about using Pa$$worD back in 1999 and I still see it today. When I worked at Wolfram Research in college, I had a password of 3.14159265358979, which I thought was ultra-secure because it was so long. I was wrong, and I received a nastygram from the company's head of security who ran a password cracker against all users, and he had cracked mine within minutes. Why? Because 3.14159265358979 is Pi and Pi was on the dictionary list of passwords to try, that's why. All well-known numbers, words and even phrases are on such lists. BeverlyHills90210 is on the list. Avogadro's number is on the list. ILoveBrunoMars is on the list. IHateBrunoMars is on the list. You can't use those for passwords.

   Many good ways are available to come up with more secure passwords, and any good cybersecurity awareness-training program will cover several. I'll cover one: Use a phrase that has meaning to you, such as "My two sons are amazing at riding and grooming horses." Take the first letter from each word to come up with Mtsaaaragh. Now replace the "t" for "two" with the number 2, capitalize the "s" in sons as if it was a proper name, and replace the "a" for "and" with the symbol &. That gets you *M2Saaar&gh*, which is a strong password. *Please don't use that example yourself.* Now that it's in print, M2Saaar&gh could make its way to hacking lists. Here is another phrase that I've used: I love to eat Oreo cookies at night. Do you? After some routine substitutions, you get: *Il2eOc@n.Du?* Surprisingly easy to remember!

Many users use the same password for every online system where they need a password. This is a problem. If one site gets hacked, cybercriminals will try your credentials at all common websites, and possibly at your business's VPN. It is imperative that your cybersecurity awareness-training program encourage your team members to use different passwords for different sites, and especially for any system that your company uses.

Finally, people have mixed opinions on how often passwords should be changed. PCI requires changes every 90 days, but many (including the FTC) now openly disagree.[83][84] I'm on the side of doing it once per year, and training your users to pick completely different passwords each year (example of what not to do: Pa$$worD1 the first year and Pa$$worD2 the next. Don't do that). Hackers will incrementally increase trailing digits. You can count on it.

2. **Implement Multi-Factor Authentication (MFA).** MFA works like this: There are three ways to identify users: something they know (a password), something they have (a car key or smartphone), or something they are (a fingerprint). Pick

two or more to identify an individual as being who they claim to be. That's MFA. In practical terms, modern MFA systems generally require a username/password (something you know) along with a *something you have* secondary means of identification, such as your smartphone. The MFA system could literally call your smartphone and ask you to press 1 if you are trying to log into the VPN, and press 2 if you are not. It can require you to open an app on your phone that makes seemingly random 6-digit codes, and you type in the 6-digit code that the app displays. The MFA system can even send a 6-digit text to your phone, although some people frown on that nowadays because texting is insecure.[85] [86] No matter how it works, a hacker has to want into your network very badly to try to get through an MFA system. Additionally, MFA systems make it much harder for your employees to share usernames and passwords, which is a good secondary benefit of implementing one. *I consider MFA even more important than the password best practices in section 1 above.*

3. **Keep your systems patched.** Remember the "WannaCry" ransomware that made worldwide news in May 2017?[1] [2] It spread quickly, in large part because it took advantage of a vulnerability that Microsoft released a fix, or "patch," for in March of that same year. In the two months since the patch came out, so many computers had not been patched that the virus had easy targets all over the world. If you had patched your computers (or just let them patch themselves via Microsoft's auto-update feature), you would have been immune from "WannaCry." Patching is important because as soon as a patch is released, hackers can reverse-engineer the patch and see exactly the vulnerability that the patch

is designed to fix. It's easy to then exploit the vulnerability on unpatched systems. That is exactly what the creators of the "WannaCry" ransomware did. Patches are available for Windows, Macs, Linux, and many other programs. Patch them. Even better, let them patch themselves. It is unusual (but not unheard of) for a patch pushed by a software company to cause side effects. However, 99% of the time, the benefits of patching vastly outweigh the risks. Within your company, talk to your server and desktop people to understand how they are patching systems. And, metrics on patching completeness are crucial. Without them, it is too easy to miss systems.

4. **Implement a cybersecurity awareness program.** If you are in manufacturing, you probably have a plant safety program. If you are a sales-focused company, you usually have extensive sales training. If you have a driver's license, you went through driver's education and had to pass a test before being allowed to drive a car. In our cyber-focused world, your staff needs to know the basics on how they can help keep your company safe. Several companies specialize in this type of training. Some companies will hire someone like me to speak to their team on real-world cybersecurity incidents as part of their "kick-off" to a cybersecurity training program. Your users are one of the most important pieces of the cybersecurity puzzle. Good technology will help a lot, but much like a car, the safest car in the world is not immune from crashing. A great deal depends upon the driver. So, your users are often the very first line of defense in your cybersecurity systems.

5. **Go through your network file shares and limit access to those that truly *need* access.** It's easy to set up a network

share, give everyone in the company full control of it, and move on. Many companies do just that. This process creates two serious problems: First, you are more likely to give people access to data they shouldn't have. Think about this from the HR perspective. Do you want payroll data for your employees accessible to everyone in the company? Second, from a cybersecurity standpoint, most ransomware looks for files that it can encrypt. If the particular user that inadvertently lets in a ransomware attack doesn't have rights to a certain set of files, the ransomware program can't reach those files. Even if a user has read-only access, ransomware can't encrypt it.

6. **Remove your users from having local administrator rights to their desktops/laptops.** This one is controversial, but I am a huge, huge advocate of it. Many companies allow their end-users to have local admin privileges on their PCs or Macs because it is easy to do so. Users can patch their own software. They can install iTunes if they want to. They can run Firefox as their web browser, even if your company installs Chrome by default. These things make users happy, and most companies like happy users. The problem is this: local admin rights also make hackers happy. If a user clicks on a malicious web link or opens an email with a bad attachment, that software will inherit the rights of that user, and a local administrator can add and remove software from their local computer whenever they wish. This represents a huge security risk to your company. **End-users, especially the CEO and other executives, should not have local admin rights to their computers.** I see many, many companies that make exceptions to this rule for executives. I believe this to be the most backwards thinking possible.

Executives are especially prone to be the victims of hacking attempts. Think about it: If you could only hack one user's email account at a company, which one would you choose? Normally the CEO or CFO. If anything, lock down your level of access and the level of access of your upper management team the most stringently of all.

7. **Outsource your email services.** This one surprises many people, and there are certain circumstances where this isn't a practical idea (see below). Companies have been running email servers internally for decades, and other companies have been outsourcing email for just as long. Why is this a cybersecurity concern? Two very important reasons:

First, email systems are very attractive for hackers. Unless you are a F1000 company, you don't have the resources that a company the size of Microsoft or Google has to keep their email systems secure and reliable. Their economy of scale and strong overall cybersecurity posture is hard to replicate, and it's in your best interest to take advantage of it.

Second, those outside of the cybersecurity community tend not to know about some important cybersecurity issues with email, but the large outsourced providers have mitigated some of these problems. Email is, by default, insecure. It's unencrypted. It goes over the Internet in clear-text, meaning that anyone who has hacked into any piece of the Internet can record any emails that get routed through the section he has hacked. The large email providers decided to take this problem on, so they exchanged encryption certificates with each other, and they encrypt all email in between each other using a technology called TLS. They then set up web interfaces that encrypt communication with their end users. *This means that if you are using an email provider such as Google, all email to other Google users or to users of other large email providers (such as Microsoft Office365) is encrypted while in motion end-to-end.* This is a very good thing, and even better, it is transparent to your users. Want to know if your outsourcing host is part of this encryption ecosystem? Check here: https://www.google.com/transparencyreport/safeemail/

If you must run your email systems internally due to concerns around auditing, implementation of preservation orders, implementation of discovery orders, records retention, the geographic location of data stores, document management, compliance with USA International Traffic in Arms Regulations (ITAR), etc., it is possible to incorporate your email services into the "automatic encryption" ecosystem described above using something called opportunistic TLS.[87] [88] It is not a guarantee of encryption, but it will encrypt your data whenever the recipient also uses an email system that supports opportunistic TLS.

8. **Whenever possible, outsource your web hosting.** Websites are to hackers what a drop of ice cream on the sidewalk is to an ant colony. Hacking websites is often how the bad guys gain a foothold into a network, and then they try to walk sideways from system to system looking for even more lucrative targets. If you can outsource this function, it's much easier to keep the bad guys out of your primary network. Some exceptions to this are: if you are running an e-commerce site that is integrated with your internal inventory system, it's hard to decouple the two. In those cases, segmenting your network as much as possible is imperative. You want to come as close as possible to having your Internet-facing systems not have any ties to your internal

network. Talk to your network team about how to do this, or find a consultant that can help you.

9. **Ensure that all your critical data is backed up, and air-gap your backups. Then do test-restores of your backups.** What is an air-gap, you ask? Good question. *An air-gap is a physical separation between a device or network and any other device or network.* A backup tape in a desk drawer is air-gapped from the Internet and from your network. By definition, an air-gapped device cannot be hacked. A bad guy can't erase it or encrypt it. After you complete a backup, your backup media needs to have an air-gap between your network and itself. Why? Because particularly nasty ransomware has figured out how to search for backup files and erase them before encrypting your production hard drives.[89] If you are using some very old-school backup methods (such as backup tapes), then the tapes that are *not* in your tape drive are air-gapped. That's decades-old methodology, though. Today, it's easiest to achieve an air-gap via portable hard drives, or by establishing a cloud backup service provider that prevents data deletion of their backups. If there isn't a single account on your network that has access to delete or edit files on your cloud provider's network, then you are reasonably close to an air-gap. Yes, it is possible to make an account that can write new data to a system, but cannot delete or modify existing data. That's what you want here.

   A word of caution: Very advanced and very patient hackers could conceivably infect your systems with a virus…and then wait. And wait. And wait until each and every one of your backups is also infected. Many companies don't keep backups beyond one year, so if a hacker is willing to wait 13 months to execute their plan, air gapped backups are not a 100% guarantee of recovering your data. It is still important to follow general cybersecurity best practices in the hopes of detecting breaches when they occur, or preventing them altogether.

10. **Have a VPN as the only external access to your internal network, and use multi-factor authentication on your VPN.** If your employees (or your internal tech staff or your outsourced managed services provider) have the ability to get to your network from home, you probably have a VPN. VPN stands for Virtual Private Network, and generally speaking, VPNs do a good job of allowing secure communication over the Internet between your network and remote locations. The problem with VPNs is that they do exactly what they are supposed to do: a VPN connection is literally the same as sitting at a desk in your office, which is something that every hacker would love to be able to do. Multi-Factor Authentication (MFA) makes it much, much harder for a hacker to gain access to your network through the VPN.

11. **Go through periodic external and internal penetration testing, and then fix those issues that are found.** Hackers get into systems by looking for weak points they can exploit. Thankfully, almost all of those weak points are already documented, and patches are available for them (or configuration changes can remove them altogether). The only weak points that are unknown are called "zero-days," and these are vulnerabilities that someone has found—but has not disclosed to the company that made the product with that vulnerability. More on those later. For known weak points, a penetration test can alert you to known issues on your network before a hacker alerts you to them in the form of a data breach or ransomware attack. Companies specialize in this type of service.

Most of the time, a penetration test on a network that has never had one before will show so many vulnerabilities that it looks overwhelming. A good security advisor can help you determine the most important ones to address.

Think of cybersecurity vulnerability remediation like a good fire-safety program: if someone is smoking next to an open gasoline can, address that issue immediately. If someone has left oily rags in a corner, it is still important to address it soon, but it's unlikely to spontaneously combust between now and lunchtime. If someone has propped open a door for five minutes while moving furniture between offices, that probably is a fire code violation and it shouldn't be ignored indefinitely, but it shouldn't be on the top of your list of issues to address either.

If you are going to have penetration testing done, it is a good idea to *have your firewall rules reviewed beforehand.* Firewalls are devices that are designed to sit between the Internet and your network, as well as in between different parts of your network. They are a critical means of keeping low-level bad guys out. I have seen so many blatant errors in firewall rules that it often makes me wonder *why more companies don't get hacked.* See my intro story for Question 11 for a real-world example. Cybersecurity consultants can help you examine firewall rules. A poorly configured firewall is very often the means that allow real-world hacks to occur, especially for companies smaller than the F1000. A firewall rule review will help reduce the number of items your penetration test reports back to you, and if the firewall is misconfigured, these might be "red-alert" issues on the penetration test report.

12. **Segment your network.** This was touched on in item 8 above, but it deserves more explanation. Segmenting a network is like installing locked doors on various rooms of your home. Most homes do not have segmented security beyond the easy-to-defeat locks on the bathrooms and bedrooms. If you get through the front door, you essentially have access to the whole home. For your computer network, this is a bad idea. If a hacker finds a way in, he can try to hack anything and everything on your network. If you divide your network into separate and distinct areas that are hard to jump between, it will help minimize the damage that a cybercriminal can do. Segments are often set up between your Internet-facing servers and your internal network (that is called a DMZ), between your Wi-Fi and wired networks, and, most importantly, between different groups/applications on your network. If you can put up network barriers between, for example, the systems that accept credit cards and those that do not, you have made a segment. If you can separate your production plant systems from your customer service systems, you have made a segment. If you can segment your SCADA systems from the rest of your network, you have made a segment. Segments make hackers' attempts to steal your data more difficult.

   Returning to the home analogy, if you viewed your home like an apartment complex, then many different people may be able to get in through the front door, but that does not mean that they have access to everything inside. This is a good thing from a cybersecurity standpoint.

   The concept of a DMZ can be taken a step further, where no computer trusts any other computer on the network unless it has been specifically programmed to do so. This is called a "zero-trust network."[13] [14] Essentially, it's a system that rejects the notion of an internal "trusted" set of computers. Much like a castle with a moat, a DMZ architecture assumes that if you got past the moat and the drawbridge, you are assumed to be a friendly person. A zero-trust network does just the opposite. The location of a computer is irrelevant. No computer is trusted by default. While this architecture takes a while to setup initially, it provides immeasurable security benefits against advanced threats. If you are in any of the high-risk categories, this is an approach that deserves serious consideration.

13. **Limit "Administrator" accounts as much as possible, and limit what each account has administrator rights to.** This one is easy to describe. If you have a master key that unlocks every office in every building that is a part of your company, your physical security hinges on that one key staying out of the hands of bad guys. If you have a separate key for each building, and even separate keys for HR, sales and technology offices, then the value of each key drops considerably. Administrator accounts can be separated in a similar fashion, where accounts that have administrator rights to your network do *not* have administrator rights to your applications. Those that do have admin rights to your applications do *not* have admin rights to your databases. You get the idea. This sort of privileged account separation will seriously slow down cybercriminals that might compromise one of these accounts, and they will also slow down insider threats as well. Microsoft has a term for this type of separation called "Red Forest."[90] [91] If your cybersecurity advisor has not heard of this term, look for an advisor that has.

14. **Implement next-generation firewalls and intrusion detection/ prevention systems.** Question 13 goes into these systems in a bit more detail, and I include them on the "blocking and

tackling" list for a simple reason. A determined bad guy will get in eventually. It's only a matter of time. You may have an internal employee go rogue and try to access things he or she shouldn't. Vulnerabilities exist in computer systems that only government agencies, organized crime cybercriminals, or individual hackers know about. These are called "zero-day" vulnerabilities, and they can't be fixed until they are known, so the bad guys choose to use these for their own purposes rather than divulge them. Remember hearing about the malicious computer worm Stuxnet back in 2010? Stuxnet was the cyberweapon that took out Iranian centrifuges used to enrich uranium. It exploited four different "zero-day" vulnerabilities, which means that whomever built Stuxnet was willing to give up a lot of their secret vulnerabilities in order to get to their target.[20] [21] [22] Our best defense against zero-days are behavioral-based detection systems, and that is what next-generation firewalls and intrusion detection/prevention systems are designed to do. These systems are far from perfect, but much like the "check engine" light on your car's dashboard, *they are better than nothing.*

15. **Log security events that occur on your network, and implement a system that reviews these logs and looks for trends.** Most of your firewalls, servers and other important infrastructure have a feature to keep a log of when they do things, or when they try to do things and they can't do them. For example, Windows server will, by default, log when someone tries to log in and does not provide a valid username and password. Imagine that on most days, a company of 100 people has 25 failed login attempts per day. That would be considered normal. Now imagine that today there were 5,000 failed login attempts. That is not normal, and is

probably the result of an active attempt to breach your company's security. This is exactly what happened during the introductory story for Question 11. *You can purchase programs that are specifically designed to look through your logs and alert a human to situations that are abnormal.* They are called Security Information and Event Management programs, or SIEM for short.[92] SIEM products can wade through the nauseatingly long logs that many of your servers and firewalls produce, and will look for things that signal something has gone off the rails. They do so as the logs are created (also called "real-time"), and as such they can do a good job of detecting a breach attempt as soon as it begins.

If your company did all 15 of the items above, you would find yourself near the top of all companies on the cybersecurity-preparedness spectrum. That is a good place to be.

QUESTIONS TO EXPLORE this topic further with your company's leaders:

> ➤ Are our systems all patched on a very regular basis?

> ➤ Do we enforce password policies for every account in our company?

> ➤ What is our cybersecurity awareness training program and why?

> ➤ Do we use encryption for sensitive data and on all portable devices?

> ➤ Do we review our lists of who has access to what data and why? How often?

HOW CAN I KEEP MYSELF EDUCATED ON CYBERSECURITY ISSUES?

"It will take a major global company going down in the wake of a cyber-attack to really shake up information security"

— ADRIAN LEPPARD, CITY OF LONDON POLICE COMMISSIONER, UK

IF YOU ARE a business owner or non-technical executive, staying on top of the latest in cybersecurity threats should be something you outsource. You need a CISO (full-time or part-time) whose job it is to stay on top of cybersecurity and bring relevant information to your attention as needed. The field changes too quickly and is too specific to certain industries or certain-sized companies for a non-technical executive to weed through the deluge of new information on cybersecurity and pick out the relevant pieces to your company. *Hire out this function.*

Your education on cybersecurity should be in the form of executive briefings. I recommend 30 minute weekly meetings with your CIO and/or CISO to update you on 1) recent events in cybersecurity, 2) on threats that have been hitting your company, and 3) the effectiveness of your cyber defenses, and 4) if cybersecurity spending is above or below budget. There could be industry-specific issues that are important for you to know.

If you take credit cards, knowing that PCI version 3.2 demands multi-factor authentication for all accounts that can access credit card data is an important piece of information.[93] If you are in the insurance industry, it is important to know that as soon as you cross $500 million in revenue, the Model Audit Rule applies to you.[94] Remember the ISAC discussion in Question 5? If you are in an industry that has an ISAC, encouraging your CISO (or a senior member of his/her team) to join and actively participate in your ISAC is a good idea. These are easy steps to take, and will go a long way in keeping your organization on top of the cyber threats it may face.

Assuming you find value in learning about cybersecurity directly, a couple of sources I recommend to my clients include:

- For in-depth reporting on important cybersecurity topics, "WIRED Magazine" does a great job. Normally they do not cover "hot-off-the-press" information, but cover really important stuff after it's been well established that it is really important.[95]

- For "hot-off-the-press" information, Brian Krebs has a reputation of being the first to break a story.[96]

- For privacy and cryptography specific topics, my friend Bruce Schneier *is the best.* Subscribe to his monthly email for fascinating information in this area. His book *Data and Goliath* is one of my favorites on how to think about privacy in our hyper-connected world.[97]

- For a monthly newsletter on trends in cybersecurity specifically written for business owners and executives, I write one free of charge. You can sign up for it at www.tcestrategy.com

Another important way to stay educated on cybersecurity issues is to form and maintain relationships with people in your geographic area that deal with cybersecurity. I try hard to be on a first-name basis with the heads of cybersecurity for the DHS, FBI and Secret Service in several cities. See the introductory story for Question 7 for an example of how very useful a strong network can be. I also have friends that are CISOs for companies in a wide variety of industries. As a business owner or executive, you might not need to know so many people in the cybersecurity arena. This is something your security professional can address. But, it never hurts to know whom these people are. When you need them, they are a phone call away. You will get a lot of pertinent information through these relationships.

QUESTIONS TO EXPLORE this topic further with your company's leaders:

> ➤ Do I have a trusted news source for cybersecurity issues that impact my company?

> ➤ Do I have a trusted advisory on cybersecurity issues?

> ➤ What resources exist within my company that I could be leveraging to keep me informed on cybersecurity?

> ➤ Are there any events I should be participating in for my own cybersecurity awareness?

NOW THAT I KNOW WHAT QUESTIONS TO ASK ABOUT CYBERSECURITY, HOW DO I KEEP THESE QUESTIONS TOP OF MIND FOR MY EXECUTIVE TEAM, AND MY COMPANY AS A WHOLE?

"If you spend more on coffee than on IT security, you will be hacked. What's more, you deserve to be hacked."
— RICHARD CLARKE, WHITE HOUSE CYBERSECURITY ADVISOR

ANY QUESTION THAT IS FORGOTTEN IS A QUESTION THAT MIGHT AS WELL HAVE NEVER BEEN ASKED AT ALL.

IT'S IMPORTANT TO make a cultural shift to embrace cybersecurity best practices if all of your new knowledge is going to produce tangible results for your company. To be honest, the media is making this task easier and easier. Cybersecurity had a front-and-center position in news headlines on a monthly basis, and enough of the population has now been impacted in some way by bad cybersecurity—such as having to replace their credit cards, having to deal with identity theft, or at a minimum dealing with unwanted emails or unwanted applications appearing on their computer from a bad mouse click. From that standpoint, we all have a head start in making good cybersecurity practices part of your company's culture.

Have you ever toured a manufacturing plant floor where signs are posted that track the number of days without a plant safety incident? How about a restroom with a sign on the door that states "Employees must wash hands before returning to work." People see these symbols every day. While these kinds of signs are never going to create 100% compliance with every best practice, they do help to keep the ideas they represent top of mind. If your industry requires, or if your company chooses to have any type of recurring training, cybersecurity training should be an integral part of teaching your employees how to be a productive member of your team.

Culture comes from the top. You are the leader (or one of the leaders) of your organization. In order to change your culture to embrace cybersecurity as one of the core requirements to have a successful business, you and your fellow leaders need to weave it into how your organization defines itself. Yes, complex passwords are a pain in the rear end, but being hacked is a much bigger pain. If you personally walk your employees through the exercise on how to create a good password that I laid out in Question 16, the odds of them taking it to heart are much higher. If you lay out cybersecurity as one of the success criteria of your upper management team—and even better, make it part of their bonus plan— the odds of your leaders incorporating cybersecurity awareness into their department are much higher.

Ideas that I have witnessed to be particularly successful include the following:

1. Have tips on cybersecurity as part of a monthly company meeting agenda. If you don't have monthly company meetings, make cybersecurity part of monthly emails that go out to your entire staff. Make them short, simple, and relevant. If you can tie them back to recent events in the news, even better.

2. Turn it into a game. Gamification—with points, rules and competition to make what could be a tedious task more fun—has taken on some traction in the workplace, and for good reason. It gets results. Offer incentives to your staff to practice good cybersecurity. Offer a $100 gift card to the person that can offer the best suggestion to improve the cybersecurity of your company without adding any expense to your bottom line (beyond the gift card).

3. Get your leadership team in on the fun. When I worked at a major bank, our compliance team began writing up team members that didn't lock their computer screens when they left their desks. So, to incent my team to take care of each other, I asked them to sit down at any desk where they found an unlocked computer, and to send an email from that computer to their entire department asking for pictures of puppies or kittens. I then asked my team to keep track of who found the most open computers, and that person could choose the food or drink for the next department meeting. Within a week, the offender rate went from over 10 incidents per day to less than one.

4. Share cybersecurity metrics with the entire company. Break down those metrics by department. If the whole company sees how many bad emails are clicked on by people in department X vs. department Y, it's going to create some competition. A little healthy competition is often a good thing.

None of these ideas are groundbreaking, but they are effective. Putting them into place starts with you and your fellow leaders.

QUESTIONS TO EXPLORE this topic further with your company's leaders:

> ➤ Are my management reviews inclusive of cyber-security concerns?

> ➤ Do I challenge my team to address cybersecurity for their departments?

> ➤ What company events do we have where cyber-security could be a theme, or at least a topic of discussion?

WHERE IS CYBERSECURITY HEADED?

"Sometimes you gotta risk."

– LT. COL. (RET.) ROB "WALDO" WALDMAN, UNITED STATES AIR FORCE

WHEN THE SOVIET Union collapsed in late 1991, my grandfather walked into the political ethics class he taught at the University of Oregon and said the following words: "The ground is littered with shards of glass from shattered crystal balls all around the world." If the future were easy to predict, stock markets would be much less volatile. Elections would be foregone conclusions. Sony would have invented the iPod. Germany would have used helium instead of hydrogen in the Hindenburg. Predicting the future is hard...

Saying that something is hard does not mean that it is impossible, though. I have had the rare opportunity to learn from futurists such as Thornton May, and based on the last 20 years of cybersecurity, I predict that the following trends will accelerate as cybersecurity permeates more and more of our everyday lives.

- **It's going to get worse before it gets better.** Much like auto-mobile safety of the mid-20th century or manufacturing safety during the Great Depression, history has taught us that there has to be a lot of carnage before substantial work is done to fix things. We need to develop fundamentally cyber-safe systems, and most of our systems today come from cyber roots where the function of the system was the only major design consideration, rather than the security and resilience of the system. This will impact your company in the following manner: Hacks are going to happen. Most of them will happen to those that take cybersecurity a little less seriously than others in the same industry. If you keep your organization a bit more cybersecure than your competition, you will have a competitive advantage when they are derailed by a cyber incident...and you are not.

- **Ransomware will become an even more prominent issue**, and companies that sell products to help build strong air-gapped backups are going to make a lot of money. Air-gapped backups are the strongest current defense against ransomware attacks, and the business model of ransomware is too strong to think that this threat will be solved anytime soon. I recommend implementing air-gapped backups.

- **The overwhelming lack of Internet-of-Things (IoT) security will continue to rear its ugly head for years to come**. There will likely be cybersecurity incidents so significant that governments take on the task of forcing manufacturers to make reasonably safe IoT devices, in a similar manner that they have with automobile or aviation safety. For now, try to find IoT devices made by manufactures that are part of the Industrial Internet Consortium, which is a group of IoT device makers that are developing, implementing and evangelizing cybersecure IoT designs.[98]

- **Critical infrastructure will be attacked, and some of those attacks will be successful.** It is very possible we will have a significant loss-of-life issue due to a cybersecurity breach. The vector could come from many angles. The water supply could be manipulated in order to sicken people. Pharmaceutical manufacturing systems could be tampered with to produce pills with far more or less dosage than they should have. Air traffic control systems may be manipulated. It is possible that there could be an automotive breach that causes braking systems to fail. As we have already seen with attacks on the Ukraine, on the Dyn DNS system and with the breaches of USA nuclear power plants,[99] cybercrime is becoming a very real threat to the infrastructure on which we depend. With any luck, a few more small-scale incidents will occur that will spur real action to protect our critical infrastructure.

- **The public cloud will soon be used by all, not just by some.** That shift will inspire significant attacks against the Internet itself in certain countries that are not liked by other countries, or by fringe groups that would prefer to watch the whole world burn. Shutting down the Internet is not merely a hypothetical concern—and I advise my larger clients to include a prolonged Internet failure as part of their disaster recovery planning exercises. As our dependence on the Internet continues to grow, the ability to attack the Internet from anywhere at any time will become a growing issue.

- **Passwords are slowly going away,** but it will be a very slow death. It will occur over decades, not years. Multi-Factor Authentication (MFA) will become the standard across all platforms, as will authentication that relies on examining the behaviors of individuals based on an Artificial Intelligence

(AI) profile. Behavioral-based cybersecurity systems will become as common as wireless Internet systems, from large businesses all the way to individual homes. I recommend that you begin implementing MFA as soon as possible.

- Speaking of AI, **AI is huge already and will get bigger.** AI techniques will be used by cybercriminals and cybersecurity firms alike in an arms race to see which side can produce an AI algorithm that can outmaneuver the other. See Question 13 for more information on how you can use AI-based cybersecurity products to help keep your company safe.

- **A LOT of private data will become public data.** Even the NSA and Sweden can't keep their secrets secret,[100][9][10] let alone private companies. Ashley Madison's client list was made public, including those that had paid extra to have their data "expunged."[101][102] A hacker purposely released a whole season of the show "Orange Is the New Black" six weeks before Netflix intended to make it public (which, arguably, did more good than harm to Netflix).[103] The concept of privacy is eroding quickly. Bruce Schneier's book, *Data and Goliath,* is a great source of information on this subject. Digital privacy will continue to erode, unless legislators are willing to stand up against corporate interests to own the data about individual citizens.

- **Skills shortages will increase.** Cybersecurity will be part of core school curricula, as is fire safety today. Even the Girl Scouts are helping fill this gap by creating 18 new cybersecurity badges that 1.8 million Girl Scouts will be able to earn.[104]

- **Quantum computing is in its infancy, but I believe that over time this technology will take off.** By smashing the speed-of-light barrier and allowing multiple solutions to be calculated simultaneously, it will break many existing forms of cryptography and will require new "quantum-safe" methodologies to replace them.[105]

- **Cybersecurity maturity scores for companies will impact the loan interest rates companies pay.** Much like FICO scores rate the creditworthiness of individuals and the big 3 Credit Rating Agencies rate the stability of investment bonds, there are already moves for similar scores that rate the maturity of the cybersecurity program any company has in place.[106] A standardized rating system will emerge for this information, and this score will directly impact companies' competitive positions in their marketspace.

- **The human element will continue to be one of the most serious causes for concern—and causes for hope around cybersecurity.** Human error will continue to account for a large number of security breaches, and human efforts will help minimize the damage done when these breaches take place. It is critical to have a strong cybersecurity awareness-training program for your organization.

- **The concept of network segmentation will expand** down to each and every device on the network. This is called a "zero trust" network (see Question 16, section 12), and there are examples of this concept that have been in use for years.[13][14] Software-defined networks that control how traffic flows between different parts of your infrastructure—based on real-time demands, current cybersecurity risks and a good dose of Artificial Intelligence—will become more mainstream.[107]

- **Cybercriminals will find new weak points in our processes to exploit**. For example, to ground large swaths of the aviation industry, there is no need to go after the airplanes. If a cybercriminal can take down the airline reservation systems used by private airlines, their planes can't fly. The takeaway here is that cybercriminals are doing *reverse incident response planning.* They are looking for areas that are critical to your business that they can exploit to harm you. You need to be looking at the same systems to devise ways to make those systems more resilient, redundant, or both.

- **More collaboration between nations.** With any luck, enough bad cybersecurity events will happen to enough governments that more collaboration between nations will emerge. I am an eternal optimist, and I'm genuinely hopeful that the adage, "the enemy of my enemy is my friend" will encourage cooperation between groups that refuse to cooperate today.

Whether or not the future of cybersecurity is bright or bleak depends in your point of view, but we can all agree on one thing: It's going to be exciting!

QUESTIONS TO EXPLORE this topic further with your company's leaders:

➤ Which cybersecurity trend is the most concerning to our company? To our industry?

➤ What are we doing to respond to that trend?

HOW CAN CYBERSECURITY BE A COMPETITIVE ADVANTAGE TO MY COMPANY?

*"We will bankrupt ourselves in the vain
search for absolute security."*

– DWIGHT D. EISENHOWER, RETIRED GENERAL AND U.S. PRESIDENT 1953–1962

WHEN I'M GIVING workshops on cybersecurity, I'm often asked to explain what I mean by "cybersecurity as a competitive advantage." Here are some examples of what I mean by this:

Which company do you think of when you think of instances where someone took on the government regarding cybersecurity and consumer privacy? Apple, that's who. Back in the 2000s, Apple was *not* thought of as a leader in consumer data protection or cybersecurity in general. Granted, they weren't known for having a huge detriment in this area, but it wasn't part of their vision they wanted to portray to the world. More recent events have changed that. Apple saw an opportunity to beef up their cybersecurity posture, and just as importantly, to advertise to consumers about their enhanced level of security. The iPhone decryption battle with the government in 2016 was a great example of this, to the point where some questioned how far was too far when it came to cybersecurity and privacy policy.[108] [109] Regardless of where you stand on the issue, it's unquestionable that Apple is working hard to have security be one of the top ten reasons that consumers should buy their products. They are not only focusing on smartphone security, either. Apple's new data storage system for their entire line of products has encryption-at-rest as its central feature.[110]

Let's switch gears to the auto industry. What one word do you think of first when I ask you to describe Volvo? Usually the first word is *safety*. They advertise their cars as being the safest in the world, and they talk about how that gives them an advantage over their competition.[111] [112] [113]

If you want to keep your anonymity online, which search engine should you use? DuckDuckGo, Inc. They specialize in offering a strong search engine without tracking your every move online.

Who makes the safest hammer in the world? The Estwing Manufacturing Company does, based in my hometown of Rockford, Illinois. Their hammers are all one piece, so it's virtually impossible for the head of the hammer to separate from the handle and become a projectile. This sort of safety-based innovation is part of what has kept their manufacturing jobs onshore since 1923.

Let's take this idea to your organization.

- If you produce a physical product, how important is the timeliness of your ability to deliver that product? Normally it's very important, and if you can get it to a buyer more quickly than your competition, you have a competitive advantage.

- If you provide a service, your ability to respond to the needs of your customers, and to give them the service they want in a timely manner, is imperative.

- If your operations are impacted less frequently by cybersecurity issues than your competition, you have a competitive advantage.

- If you are in an industry where privacy of your customers' information is important—which includes more and more companies, as regulations like GDPR take hold—you can even use your cybersecurity program as a sales tool.

If Apple can creatively use cybersecurity as a competitive advantage, so can your company. Even if you aren't in a business where cybersecurity is generally thought of as a true differentiator between vendors, you can still tip the tables in your favor. If you have a more-robust cybersecurity and disaster recovery program than your competitor, you might be more willing than your competitor to sign a contract with a client that includes stiffer penalties to you if you can't meet certain service-level agreements in the contract. This makes you a more attractive vendor, which is the heart of a competitive advantage.

Sometimes people ask if it's a *mistake* to bring up cybersecurity to customers because it could plant a seed in their mind that associates your product or service with cybersecurity incidents. I'll be blunt: that is antiquated thinking. Between the 2014 Anthem healthcare breach, the 2015 Office of Personnel Management breach, the 2016 USA election hacking allegations, and the "WannaCry" ransomware issue of 2017, the media has already planted that seed in consumers' minds. It's up to you to address the already-planted seed with your customers in a positive light, rather than ignore it altogether.

A difficult loss to quantify is the loss of competitive advantage. Remember the example from Question 1 on the acquisition gone wrong due to hacking of an email server? The company being acquired lost a critical advantage in the negotiation process, and it became unrecoverable. If your competition gets hold of your new product plans and releases a copycat product ahead of yours, it could change the fundamental course of your business.

Extreme examples, but we know real-world instances of each one. Generally speaking, the *business disruption aspect* of breaches is the most damaging. *Damage to your reputation* is smaller, more temporary, and can be mitigated with a good public relations strategy. *Fines* from regulatory bodies have been relatively small overall.

One of the largest competitive advantages that any company can have is the trust of its customers. Customers that trust your organization are less concerned about price, and are more tolerant of glitches or small issues. They are more loyal to you when a new competitor emerges. Trust drives emotion and emotion drives buying behavior. Without trust, many organizations don't stand a chance. Keeping your company resilient from cyber-attack instills a level of trust that is more and more advantageous to your organization. With each passing headline of company X, Y and Z falling victim to a cybersecurity breach, those that have not gain a leg up on the trust your customers have in you.

Trust drives emotion and emotion drives buying behavior.

However, a large silver lining exists in all of this. When a company does good planning for a potential disaster, such as a tornado, earthquake or snowstorm, the damage from such an event is likely reduced. That's the whole point of planning. However, *the likelihood of the event itself taking place is completely outside of the company's control.* Just because you have the best possible planning for an earthquake makes you no more or less likely to be hit by one (unless you are a subscriber to Murphy's Law, and I'm not). Good preparation for bad weather doesn't change the weather forecast…

Cybersecurity planning is exactly the opposite. Good preparation dramatically increases your odds of not only weathering a cybersecurity storm, but of preventing one in the first place. It will be a significant undertaking to take a good hard look at the 20 cybersecurity questions in this book and apply them to your company. The reward for doing so will be enormous, as you will dramatically stack the cards in your favor so that a breach happens to your competitors—and not to you.

Stay safe!

QUESTIONS TO EXPLORE this topic further with your company's leaders:

> ➤ Is cybersecurity becoming a competitive differentiator in our industry? Could it be a differentiator for us?

> ➤ What are we doing to embrace cybersecurity as a means to bring competitive advantage?

ACRONYMS

A/C: Air Conditioning

BAA: Business Associate Agreement. A BAA is a requirement of HIPAA for vendors that do business with a HIPAA compliant company. The vendor needs to store, process or have access to data protected by HIPAA regulations in order for the BAA to apply.

CEO: Chief Executive Officer

CFO: Chief Financial Officer

CIO: Chief Information Officer

CISO: Chief Information Security Officer

COBIT: Control Objectives for Information and Related Technologies. Cybersecurity framework.

COO: Chief Operating Officer

CRM: Customer Relationship Management: A system to track customer interactions. Sometimes the line between a CRM system and an ERP system gets fuzzy. Don't worry about it. Think of these systems as the "gears" of a large machine, and the company using it is that machine.

DFARS: Defense Federal Acquisition Regulation Supplement

DHS: USA Department of Homeland Security

DMZ: DeMilitarized Zone. This is a part of a network that faces the Internet on one side and internal network(s) on the other side. Best practice is to limit the traffic that can traverse a DMZ as much as possible.

DNS: Domain Name Servers. These are the servers that translate website names such as www.bryceaustin.com to IP addresses such as 107.180.27.156

ERP: Enterprise Resource Planning. Normally a large software system designed to aid a manufacturing, healthcare or retail company. The ERP system tracks their orders, their supply chain, their raw materials, items in transit, and so on.

EU: European Union

F1000: Fortune 1000. Largest 1000 publicly traded companies in the USA

FBI: Federal Bureau of Investigation

FTC: Federal Trade Commission

FTP: File Transfer Protocol. Insecure. Sends usernames and passwords in clear text across the Internet. Invented in 1971, back before security on the Internet was a concern, mostly because the Internet didn't really exist by today's standards.[114] Avoid like the plague.

GDPR: General Data Protection Regulation. Data Privacy and retention regulations covering the EU.

HIPAA: Health Insurance Portability and Accountability Act

HITRUST: Health Information Trust Alliance

HR: Human Resources

Hyper-V: Microsoft's software platform to virtualize multiple servers on a single physical server. Hyper-V used to be called Windows Server Virtualization.

ID: Identification. For example, if you want to board a plane, be prepared to show ID.

IoT: Internet of Things. All the devices that are connected to the Internet but don't traditionally fall under the category of "computer." Internet-connected thermostats, security cameras, refrigerators and hearing aids are IoT devices.

IP: Internet Protocol. This is one of the fundamental definitions that describes how information flows from one computer to another, or from one remote end of the Internet to another.

ISAC: Information Sharing and Analysis Centers. These are the groups that companies in many different industries can join to exchange information on cybersecurity.

ISACA: Information Systems Audit and Control Association. ISACA is responsible for certifications such as the CISM and CISA, and wrote the COBIT cybersecurity framework.

ISO: International Standards Organization

IT: Information Technology

ITAR: International Traffic in Arms Regulations. A USA regulatory regime to restrict and control the export of defense and military related technologies to safeguard national security.

MCP: Microsoft Certified Professional

MFA: Multi Factor Authentication. You can identify someone as being who he claims to be in one of three ways: Something he knows (a password), something he has (a car key), or something he is (a fingerprint). MFA requires that you pick two or more different types to authenticate someone. This is a very effective means of deterring hackers.

MLAT: Mutual Legal Assistance Treaty. This is when the governments of different countries agree to help each other fight criminal activity across their borders.

NIST: National Institute of Standards and Technology

NSA: National Security Agency. They head up cryptology for the US government.

OPM: Office of Personnel Management. This is the US government's HR department.

OSHA: Occupational Safety and Health Administration

PC: Personal Computer

PCI: Payment Card Industry

PHI: Protected Health Information. There are 18 types of data protected by HIPAA, and they are collectively known as Protected Health Information.

RPO: Recovery Point Objective. The amount of time since your last data backup. This does not refer to how long it takes you to restore your last backup, but rather how long has gone by since you had a backup.

RTO: Recovery Time Objective. The amount of time that can pass before a system comes back online. This does not refer to the age of the data the system contains, but rather whether or not a system is available to be used.

SCADA: Supervisory Control And Data Acquisition. These are the systems that control things like manufacturing plants, water treatment plants and even nuclear energy plants. They are important for cybersecurity because they often have security vulnerabilities in them, and if those vulnerabilities are exploited, they could cause serious damage to the system they control.

SFTP: Secure File Transfer Protocol. A secure replacement for FTP. Another variant is called FTPS. FTPS and SFTP are different from a technical standpoint, but both are leaps and bounds better than FTP.

SIEM: Security Information and Event Management. These are systems that are designed to examine the logs that your technology systems produce in real-time, and provide alerts on events that may indicate a security breach or attempted breach. They can be sold as a piece of software, as a stand-alone appliance, or as a managed service.

SLA: Service Level Agreement. This is an agreement with a vendor on how soon they need to deliver their product or service. Typically SLAs cover things like maximum downtime, response to issues, etc.

SOC: Security Operations Center. Also called ISOC (Information Security Operations Center). This is where intelligence about potential cyber threats is collected, analyzed and acted upon. Smaller companies tend to outsource SOC services, and larger ones may have a SOC in-house.

SSL: Secure Socket Layer. This used to be the standard security technology for establishing an encrypted link between a web server and a browser. As with most technologies, vulnerabilities were found in SSL, and TLS has replaced it as the default security standard for websites.

TLS: Transport Layer Security. Replacement for SSL.

TV: Television

UK: United Kingdom

US/USA: United States of America

VPN: Virtual Private Network

VW: Volkswagen

WSJ: Wall Street Journal

And

TCE Strategy: That's the company I founded to help other companies with their technology and cybersecurity vision, strategy and execution. TCE stands for Technology and Cybersecurity Education.

APPENDIX: MORE DETAILS ON CYBERSECURITY REGULATIONS AND FRAMEWORKS

"Without data, you are just someone with an opinion."
– MILES EDMUNDSON, CISO, CERIDIAN

CYBERSECURITY FRAMEWORKS:

NIST (NATIONAL INSTITUTE of Standards and Technology): The NIST group has been working to bring standards to the scientific area for over 100 years. Want to know how to measure the length of a bridge truss? How do you measure the correct dose of medicine to give a patient? How strong is a steel pipe? NIST helps make these things a reality.

The NIST standards are broken into two distinct areas: 1) NIST 800-53, which is a set of detailed security controls for federal information systems, and 2) a more general cybersecurity framework. The framework was designed in response to Executive Order #13636 issued in 2013, which was a call to "improve critical infrastructure cybersecurity."[115] It outlines 5 core cybersecurity activities (Identify, Protect, Detect, Respond and Recover), along with 4 different tiers of maturity that an organization can have within each activity. For many organizations, the NIST framework is a very good place to begin a cybersecurity program. In 2017, a new executive order was signed which requires the heads of all US government agencies to "be guided by the NIST Framework for Improving Critical Infrastructure Cybersecurity."[35] NIST is completely free to use, and is offered up by the US government in the hopes that it will serve the common good.

ISO 27000 (International Standards Organization):[36] We all need to agree on some things. Everyone is better served if we pick a standard and stick to it. For example, if we are in the same time zone, all of our clocks (in theory) agree on what time it is right now. We also all need to agree on where time zones begin and end. What country code do I use to mail a package? It's important for the whole world to agree on that. ISO handles these things. From food production safety standards to general risk management frameworks, ISO has you covered. If you are in manufacturing, you are probably familiar with the ISO 9000 set of quality management standards. The smart people at the ISO have come up with a set of frameworks for information security management, known as ISO 27000.[37] Its look and feel is similar to NIST, but NIST was developed with the US in mind, and ISO is more global in scope. If you are doing a lot of worldwide business, ISO 27000 may be a better choice than NIST, but to be honest, most of both frameworks are interchangable.[38] Finally, ISO charges fees to use its publications, whereas NIST is free to use.

COBIT (Control Objectives for Information and Related Technology): COBIT has been around in one form or another since the mid 1990's. It is an IT process and governance framework developed by ISACA, the Information Systems Audit and Control Association. COBIT is broad. Very broad. Broad as in mouth-of-the-Mississippi-River broad. The latest version is COBIT 5, and it has (shockingly) 5 pillars:

- Audit and Assurance

- Risk Management

- Information Security

- Regulatory and Compliance

- Governance of Enterprise IT

COBIT is the kind of framework that is used to implement other frameworks across an organization. It contains several articles on how to implement NIST 800-53 (see above) using the COBIT model. Sometimes an incestuous relationship exists between cybersecurity frameworks. For larger organizations, COBIT is a great way to have "one ring to rule them all" when it comes to your regulatory, cybersecurity, compliance and governance systems.

FULL DISCLOSURE: I hold a CISM (Certified Information Security Manager) certification from ISACA.

CYBERSECURITY LAWS/DIRECTIVES:

PCI (Payment Card Industry): Do you take credit cards? Well, those companies that issue credit cards have come up with an exhaustingly descriptive set of cybersecurity standards that you are supposed to comply with if you accept credit cards. To be honest, most of them are good ideas, but a few of them are virtually impossible to comply with. For example, PCI requirement 5.1.1 states that your antivirus software must "Detect all known types of malicious software, remove all known types of malicious software, and protect against all known types of malicious software." No one makes that product. No one will ever make that product. If such a product did exist, it might give so many false positives that your employees would threaten mutiny. PCI is also an "all-or-nothing" system: if you fail even a single control, you fail compliance.

If you look past the imperfections, though, most of PCI makes a lot of sense. Not a bad choice on which to base a cybersecurity program. If you take credit cards and are not PCI compliant, you could be fined by the PCI board, or even be banned from accepting credit cards altogether. Truth be told, to my knowledge the "nuclear option" of banning a retailer from taking credit cards due strictly to PCI non-compliance has never been exercised. Regrettably, many companies take the approach to try to limit the scope of PCI to the specific areas of their company that store or transmit credit cards, which leaves many other important systems more vulnerable to hackers.

Compliance with PCI is voluntary. PCI is not a law. It is a directive from those that offer and process credit cards.

HIPAA (Health Insurance Portability and Accountability Act): HIPAA started with such good intentions. Dating back to 1996, HIPAA was designed to ensure that individuals would be able to maintain health insurance coverage between jobs, and it also set standards to ensure the security and confidentiality of patient information.[39] In 2009, HITECH (Health Information Technology for Economic and Clinical Health) was tacked on top of HIPAA to add individuals as covered entities and to lay out breach notification procedures. More recently, a group of large healthcare companies (including Anthem, who currently holds the title for the largest healthcare breach in history) have put together their own cybersecurity framework called HITRUST that is designed to combine framework components from most of the popular ones into one big ball, similar to COBIT.[116]

HIPAA has 18 separate "identifiers" that are considered Protected Health Information (PHI):

1. Names

2. Address (including zip code)

3. Dates (birth, admission, discharge, death)

4. Telephone numbers

5. Fax numbers

6. E-mail addresses

7. Social security numbers

8. Medical record numbers

9. Health plan beneficiary numbers

10. Account numbers

11. Certificate/License numbers

12. Vehicle identifiers and serial numbers (including license plate)

13. Device identifiers and serial numbers

14. Web Universal Resource Locators (URLs)

15. Internet Protocol (IP) addresses

16. Biometric identifiers, including finger and voice prints

17. Full-face photographic images and any comparable images, and

18. Any other unique identifying number, characteristic, or code

HIPAA is a very subjective standard relative to others. For example, HIPAA requires that, "reasonable precautions should be used to avoid sharing patient information with those not involved in the patient's care," but the definition of "reasonable" is left as an exercise to the reader. Over time many of the requirements have become easier to interpret, often as the result of litigation.

HIPAA is not just a set of guidelines. This is an Act of Congress. Compliance is mandatory. HIPAA has teeth: You must report a breach within 60 days, both to individuals impacted and to the government. You must operate your business with employees having the "minimum necessary" access to PHI data. Civil penalties range from $100 to $50,000 per incident and up to $1.5 million per year. Criminal penalties range from $50,000 to $250,000 and 1–10 years in jail. People have done serious jail time over HIPAA violations.[40]

Take HIPAA seriously. Because HIPAA centers on the healthcare industry, it is normally used as a cybersecurity standard only by those handling PHI data.

DFARS (Defense Federal Acquisition Regulation Supplement): Do you do any work with the United States Department of Defense? If so, you should already know about DFARS.[41] What you may not know is that there is a section specifically addressing cybersecurity and rules around disclosing data breaches.[42] If you are in this industry or are considering joining this industry, I recommend going to the citations section of this book and reading up on these rules.

GDPR (General Data Protection Regulation): Do you do business within any European Union (EU) countries? Do you have any data at all on citizens of a EU country? If you do, GDPR is a big deal.[43] GDPR focuses on protecting data *and controlling how you can use it* for anyone in the EU. You must get consent before collecting personal data. You must appoint a Data Privacy Officer for your company. You must do Privacy Impact Assessments. You must notify a "data protection authority" of a data breach within three days of discovering it—interesting to note: HIPAA allows 60 days. GDPR gives people *the right to be forgotten*, meaning you must be able to purge your data of any trace of a citizen upon request. Again, GDPR is a fundamental requirement if you have employees, customers or suppliers in the EU. It applies to all firms handling data on EU citizens, even if the country where a supplier is based is outside the EU. If it applies to you, take it seriously.

NOTE: GDPR has a different twist than the other regulations in this section. It focuses on privacy protection, and as such it has requirements that go beyond "traditional" cybersecurity concerns. Penalties for violating GDPR vary widely on the size/scope of the penalty, but worst case, it's 20 million Euros or 4% of a company's global annual turnover, whichever is greater. Ouch!

Which one of the above cybersecurity frameworks is best for you? There isn't an easy answer, and often multiple frameworks will impact your core business. As an example, many universities have a health clinic on campus, and its technology systems must comply to HIPAA. If the campus bookstore or cafeteria takes credit cards, those systems must comply with PCI.

The campus admissions department must comply with GDPR if EU students ever apply to the university. *The core takeaway is that you may have no choice but to comply with some requirements, and you may have the option to utilize others as tools on which to base your cybersecurity program on.* This is a complicated decision. The best framework(s) for you depend on your industry, your geography, your size, the type of data you use to run your business, and any existing contracts you have with clients or future contracts you hope to win. It is important to pick a framework or frameworks that makes sense for your organization and to devise a plan to adopt those procedural and technical best practices.

Answering this question for your specific situation is one of the things that a good cybersecurity advisor can help you accomplish.

LIST OF QUESTIONS FOR YOUR COMPANY'S LEADERSHIP TEAM

Chapters Review Questions for Your Company's Leadership Team

FROM QUESTION 1: Why Is Cybersecurity a Problem for My Company?

> ➤ What is our liability if a cybersecurity incident causes a production outage or a data exposure?

> ➤ What regulatory concerns do we have if a breach occurs?

FROM QUESTION 2: Where Is My Data, and How Can I Keep It Secure?

> ➤ What sensitive data does your department create, consume and store?

> ➤ What protections exist to keep that data secure?

> ➤ Who determines where your department's data sits, both inside the company and outside?

> ➤ Who determines who gets access to which data?

FROM QUESTION 3: How Valuable a Target Is My Company to Cybercriminals?

➤ Who in our industry has been hit by cybersecurity incidents?

➤ What commodity data do we possess that is valuable on the black market?

➤ What is the total value of our data if it were to hit the dark web?

➤ How much would we be willing to pay if someone was to shut down our business with a cyberattack?

FROM QUESTION 4: Who Are These Cybercriminals?

➤ Is our organization a target for Nation State level attacks? Are we part of critical infrastructure, are we known as a leader in our industry, or are we in a type of business that other countries may object to?

➤ Do we do business in a country where we may be caught in the crossfire of Nation State attacks?

FROM QUESTION 5: Why Isn't Law Enforcement Doing More About Cybercrime?

➤ Do we know our Federal and local representatives for cybercrime prevention?

➤ What is our policy on when we reach out to these agencies? Who has the authority to make that decision?

FROM QUESTION 6: Who is Responsible for Cybersecurity Concerns at My Company?

➤ Do we have a policy on who can proactively shut down systems based on a concern of cybersecurity risk?

➤ Who is the decision maker on if an incident is a cybersecurity issue?

FROM QUESTION 7: What Is the First Call I Should Make if My Team Suspects a Breach?

➤ Do we have a playbook on how we investigate suspected cybersecurity incidents?

➤ What is our communication and escalation process on suspected incidents?

FROM QUESTION 8: What Do My Employees Need to Know About Cybersecurity?

➤ When was the last time you were trained on cybersecurity? What did you take away from it?

➤ Do your team members who have access to sensitive data get additional training above and beyond those who do not?

FROM QUESTION 9: What Standards or Regulations for Cybersecurity Should My Company Use as the Basis for a Cybersecurity Program?

➤ What regulations is our company required to follow due to our industry?

➤ What regulations is our company required to follow due to our geography?

➤ What cybersecurity framework(s) do we find useful for our business?

➤ Where are we on implementation and practice maturity of the framework(s) we choose to follow?

FROM QUESTION 10: How Much Would My Customers Care About a Cybersecurity Breach?

➤ How important is customer trust to our brand?

➤ Do our competitors try to differentiate themselves based on trust?

➤ What is it that we must protect to maintain our customers' trust?

FROM QUESTION 11: What Is My Playbook if I Have a Cybersecurity Incident?

➤ How do we test our incident response playbook?

➤ How often do we test it?

➤ What did we learn from our last test?

FROM QUESTION 12: How Do I Know if My Incident-Response Plan Is Going to Work the Way It Should?

➤ How does our company assess the success or failure of an incident response test?

➤ When was the last time a test was done and what were the findings?

➤ Which systems would shut down our business if we lost them?

➤ Has our incident response plan even been run by someone outside of the technology team to ensure that the leader in this department isn't the only person that can execute it?

FROM QUESTION 13: What Are All These "Next-Generation Firewalls," "Intrusion Prevention Systems," and "Security as a Service" Systems That People Are Trying to Sell My Company?

➤ Do we have the right tools to detect cyberattacks?

➤ Do we have the right tools and vendor partners to react to a cyberattack?

➤ Do we have the right tools to protect against cyberattacks?

➤ Do we have trusted partners to help us make the best decisions on the tools above?

FROM QUESTION 14: Do Our Vendors Care if They Cause a Breach of Our Data?

➤ Do our contracts have language on cybersecurity?

➤ What penalties or liabilities do we ask from our vendors in our contracts?

➤ Which of our vendors have access to our sensitive data, and how do those vendor contracts differ from others?

FROM QUESTION 15: What Is All This "Internet of Things" Stuff I Have Been Hearing About?

➤ What IoT devices exist within our company and why?

➤ How many total devices are attached to our networks?

➤ How do we know that the devices on our networks have a reasonable level of cybersecurity?

FROM QUESTION 16: Are There "Blocking-and-Tackling" Things That I Should Be Doing Around Cybersecurity?

➤ Are our systems all patched on a very regular basis?

➤ Do we enforce password policies for every account in our company?

➤ What is our cybersecurity awareness training program and why?

➤ Do we use encryption for sensitive data and on all portable devices?

➤ Do we review our lists of who has access to what data and why? How often?

FROM QUESTION 17: How Can I Keep Myself Educated on Cybersecurity Issues?

➤ Do I have a trusted news source for cybersecurity issues that impact my company?

➤ Do I have a trusted advisory on cybersecurity issues?

➤ What resources exist within my company that I could be leveraging to keep me informed on cybersecurity?

➤ Are there any events I should be participating in for my own cybersecurity awareness?

FROM QUESTION 18: Now That I Know What Questions to Ask About Cybersecurity, How Do I Keep These Questions top of Mind for My Executive Team, and My Company as a Whole?

➤ Are my management reviews inclusive of cybersecurity concerns?

> ➤ Do I challenge my team to address cybersecurity for their departments?

> ➤ What company events do we have where cybersecurity could be a theme, or at least a topic of discussion?

FROM QUESTION 19: Where Is Cybersecurity Headed?

> ➤ Which cybersecurity trend is the most concerning to our company? To our industry?

> ➤ What are we doing to respond to that trend?

FROM QUESTION 20: How Can Cybersecurity Be a Competitive Advantage to My Company?

> ➤ Is cybersecurity becoming a competitive differentiator in our industry? Could it be a differentiator for us?

> ➤ What are we doing to embrace cybersecurity as a means to bring competitive advantage?

ABOUT THE AUTHOR

BRYCE AUSTIN STARTED his technology career on a Commodore 64 computer and a cassette tape drive. Today he is a leading voice on emerging technology and cybersecurity issues. Bryce holds a CISM certification and is known as a thought leader, cybersecurity authority, and internationally recognized professional speaker.

With over 10 years of experience as a Chief Information Officer and Chief Information Security Officer, Bryce actively advises company boards in industries as diverse as financial services, retail, healthcare, technology and manufacturing. He was the CIO and CISO of Wells Fargo Business Payroll Services, and a Senior Group Manager at Target Corporation. He has first-hand experience of what happens to a business and its employees during a cybersecurity crisis, as it did to Target because of their 2013/2014 credit card data breach.

When Bryce isn't spending quality time with his wife and two young sons, he spends his weekends as a high-speed track driver and coach at venues across the USA. He has over 15 years of experience, and has driven cars as diverse as an 85 horsepower Saturn to a 650 horsepower Porsche 911 Turbo. He has had more than 100 students under his instruction, all alive and eager to drive again.

CITATIONS

1. Roy, Mekhala. 2017. *WannaCry ransomware attack: Dry those tears and get back to basics.* 5 19. Accessed 8 28, 2017. http://searchcio.techtarget.com/news/450419229/WannaCry-ransomware-attack-Dry-those-tears-and-get-back-to-basics.

2. Pham, Sherisse. 2017. *What is ransomware?* 6 28. Accessed 8 28, 2017. http://money.cnn.com/2017/05/15/technology/ransomware-wannacry-explainer/.

3. Goel, Vindu. 2017. *One Billion Yahoo Accounts Still for Sale, Despite Hacking Indictments.* 3 17. Accessed 8 28, 2017. https://www.nytimes.com/2017/03/17/technology/yahoo-hack-data-indictments.html.

4. Reisch, Marc S. 2012. *China Accused Of Stealing DuPont Trade Secrets.* 2 9. Accessed 8 28, 2017. http://cen.acs.org/articles/90/web/2012/02/China-Accused-Stealing-DuPont-Trade.html.

5. Wilber, Del Quentin. 2016. *How a corporate spy swiped plans for DuPont's billion-dollar color formula.* 2 4. Accessed 8 28, 2017. https://www.bloomberg.com/features/2016-stealing-dupont-white/

6. Hawkins, Brett. 2015. *Case Study: The Home Depot Data Breach.* 1 2. Accessed 8 28, 2017. https://www.sans.org/reading-room/whitepapers/casestudies/case-study-home-depot-data-breach-36367.

7. McGee, Marianne Kolbasuk. 2017. *A New In-Depth Analysis of Anthem Breach.* 1 10. Accessed 8 28, 2017. http://www.bankinfosecurity.com/new-in-depth-analysis-anthem-breach-a-9627.

8. Overfelt, Maggie. 2016. *The next big threat in hacking — data sabotage.* 3 9. Accessed 8 28, 2017. http://www.cnbc.com/2016/03/09/the-next-big-threat-in-hacking—data-sabotage.html.

9. Khandelwal, Swati. 2017. *Sweden Accidentally Leaks Personal Details of Nearly All Citizens.* 7 24. Accessed 8 29, 2017. http://thehackernews.com/2017/07/sweden-data-breach.html.

10. The Local SE. 2017. Swedish cyber security slip-up 'a complete failure': PM Stefan Löfven. 7 24. Accessed 8 29, 2017. https://www.thelocal.se/20170724/swedish-cyber-security-slip-up-a-disaster-pm-stefan-lofven.

11. Wikipedia. 2017. Coca-Cola formula. 8 25. Accessed 8 29, 2017. https://en.wikipedia.org/wiki/Coca-Cola_formula.

12. Koerner, Brendan I. 2016. *Inside the Cyberattack That Shocked the US Government.* 10 23. Accessed 8 29, 2017. https://www.wired.com/2016/10/inside-cyberattack-shocked-us-government/.

13. Armasu, Lucian. 2015. *Google Adopts Zero Trust Network Model For Its Own Cloud.* 5 13. Accessed 8 29, 2017. http://www.tomsitpro.com/articles/google-zerotrust-network-own-cloud,1-2608.html.

14. Asay, Matt. 2017. *The best security? Have Zero Trust, says expert.* 5 11. Accessed 8 29, 2017. http://www.techrepublic.com/article/the-best-security-have-zero-trust-says-expert/.

15. Herman, Bob. 2016. *Details of Anthem's massive cyberattack remain in the dark a year later.* 3 30. Accessed 8 28, 2017. http://www.modernhealthcare.com/article/20160330/NEWS/160339997.

16. Crowe, Jonathan. 2017. *2017 Ransomware Trends and Forecasts.* 2. Accessed 8 29, 2017. https://blog.barkly.com/new-ransomware-trends-2017.

17. Wikipedia. 2017. *Sony Pictures hack.* 8 25. Accessed 8 29, 2017. https://en.wikipedia.org/wiki/Sony_Pictures_hack.

18. Chappell, Bill. 2017. *'Petya' Ransomware Hits At Least 65 Countries; Microsoft Traces It To Tax Software.* 6 28. Accessed 8 29, 2017. http://www.npr.org/sections/thetwo-way/2017/06/28/534679950/petya-ransomware-hits-at-least-65-countries-microsoft-traces-it-to-tax-software.

19. Financial Times. 2017. *DLA Piper still struggling with Petya cyber attack.* Accessed 8 29, 2017. https://www.ft.com/content/1b5f863a-624c-11e7-91a7-502f7ee26895.

20. Zetter, Kim. 2011. *How Digital Detectives Deciphered Stuxnet, the Most Menacing Malware in History.* 7 11. Accessed 8 29, 2017. https://www.wired.com/2011/07/how-digital-detectives-deciphered-stuxnet/.

21. Zetter, Kim. 2015. *THE NSA ACKNOWLEDGES WHAT WE ALL FEARED: IRAN LEARNS FROM US CYBERATTACKS.* 2 10. Accessed 8 29, 2017. https://www.wired.com/2015/02/nsa-acknowledges-feared-iran-learns-us-cyberattacks/.

22. Naraine, Ryan. 2010. *Stuxnet attackers used 4 Windows zero-day exploits.* 9 14. Accessed 8 29, 2017. http://www.zdnet.com/article/stuxnet-attackers-used-4-windows-zero-day-exploits/.

23. Identity Management Institute. 2016. *Employee Errors Cause Most Data Breach Incidents in Cyber Attacks.* 10 12. Accessed 8 29, 2017. http://www.prnewswire.com/news-releases/employee-errors-cause-most-data-breach-incidents-in-cyber-attacks-300342879.html.

24. Ashford, Warwick. 2015. *Data classification key to IP protection, says Titus.* 5 29. Accessed 8 29, 2017. http://www.computerweekly.com/news/4500247170/Data-classification-key-to-IP-protection-says-Titus.

25. van Zadelhoff, Marc. 2016. *The Biggest Cybersecurity Threats Are Inside Your Company.* 9 16. Accessed 8 29, 2017. https://hbr.org/2016/09/the-biggest-cybersecurity-threats-are-inside-your-company.

26. Seals, Tara. 2016. *Annual Cybercrime Costs to Double to $6 Trillion by 2021.* 1 9. Accessed 8 29, 2017. https://www.infosecurity-magazine.com/news/annual-cybercrime-costs-double-6/.

27. U.S. State Department. 2014. *Treaties, Agreements, and Asset Sharing.* Accessed 8 28, 2017. https://www.state.gov/j/inl/rls/nrcrpt/2014/vol2/222469.htm.

28. U.S. Department of Homeland Security. *Cybersecurity.* Accessed 8 28, 2017. https://www.dhs.gov/topic/cybersecurity.

29. Congress.gov. 2016. *S.754 - To improve cybersecurity in the United States through enhanced sharing of information about cybersecurity threats, and for other purposes.* Accessed 8 29, 2017. https://www.congress.gov/bill/114th-congress/senate-bill/754.

30. U.S. government, Department of Homeland Security. *Find a Field Office.* Accessed 8 28, 2017. https://www.secretservice.gov/contact/field-offices/.

31. U.S. government, Federal Bureau of Investigation. *Field Offices.* Accessed 8 28, 2017. https://www.fbi.gov/contact-us/field-offices.

32. InfraGard, *Welcome to InfraGard.* Accessed 8 28, 2017. https://www.infragard.org/.

33. National Council of ISACs. 2016. *Member ISACS.* Accessed 8 28, 2017. https://www.nationalisacs.org/member-isacs.

34. Wikipedia. 2017. *Sarbanes–Oxley Act.* 8 27. Accessed 8 29, 2017. https://en.wikipedia.org/wiki/Sarbanes%E2%80%93Oxley_Act.

35. Klein Murillo, Helen. 2017. *A Summary of the Cybersecurity Executive Order.* 5 11. Accessed 8 29, 2017. https://www.lawfareblog.com/summary-cybersecurity-executive-order.

36. International Organization for Standardization. *ISO/IEC 27000 family - Information security management systems.* Accessed 8 29, 2017. https://www.iso.org/isoiec-27001-information-security.html.

37. Wikipedia. 2017. *ISO/IEC 27000-series.* 8 19. Accessed 8 29, 2017. https://en.wikipedia.org/wiki/ISO/IEC_27000-series.

38. Secuilibrium, LLC. 2014. *Comparing NIST's Cybersecurity Framework with ISO/IEC 27001.* 2 14. Accessed 8 29, 2017. http://www.secuilibrium.com/news/comparing-isoiec-27001-with-nists-cybersecurity-framework.

39. University of Chicago Medical Center. 2010. *HIPAA BACKGROUND.* 2. Accessed 8 28, 2017. http://hipaa.bsd.uchicago.edu/background.html.

40. Kolbasuk McGee, Marianne. 2015. *Prison Term in HIPAA Violation Case.* 2 20. Accessed 8 29, 2017. http://www.inforisktoday.com/prision-term-in-hipaa-violation-case-a-7938.

41. Defense Procurement and Acquisition Policy. 2017. *Defense Federal Acquisition Regulation Supplement (DFARS) and Procedures, Guidance, and Information (PGI).* 1 10. Accessed 8 29, 2017. http://www.acq.osd.mil/dpap/dars/dfarspgi/current/.

42. Defense Procurement and Acquisition Policy. 2016. *SUBPART 204.73— SAFEGUARDING COVERED DEFENSE INFORMATION AND CYBER INCIDENT REPORTING.* 10 21. Accessed 8 29, 2017. http://www.acq.osd.mil/dpap/dars/dfars/html/current/204_73.htm.

43. EU General Data Protection Regulation Portal. *GDPR Portal: Site Overview* Accessed 8 29, 2017. http://www.eugdpr.org/.

44. Roman, Jeffrey. 2014. *Neiman Marcus Downsizes Breach Estimate.* 2 23. Accessed 8 28, 2017. http://www.bankinfosecurity.com/neiman-marcus-downsizes-breach-estimate-a-6532.

45. Wolfson, Tina. 2017. *Hilary Remijas, et. al. vs The Neiman Marcus Group, LLC, Case: 1:14-cv-01735 Document #: 148, PLAINTIFFS' AMENDED MOTION*

FOR PRELIMINARY APPROVAL OF CLASS ACTION SETTLEMENT AND CERTIFICATION OF SETTLEMENT CLASS. 3 17. Accessed 8 28, 2017. https://consumermediallc.files.wordpress.com/2017/03/n-d-ill-_null_null_0.pdf.

46. Wahba, Phil. 2017. *Neiman Marcus Puts Itself Up for Sale As Business Shrivels.* 3 14. Accessed 8 28, 2017. http://fortune.com/2017/03/14/neiman-marcus-sale/.

47. Sidel, Robin. 2014. *Home Depot's 56 Million Card Breach Bigger Than Target's.* 9 18. Accessed 8 28, 2017. https://www.wsj.com/articles/home-depot-breach-bigger-than-targets-1411073571.

48. Reuters, 2016. *Home Depot Will Pay $19.5 Million After Major 2014 Data Breach.* 3 9. Accessed 8 29, 2017. http://www.nbcnews.com/business/business-news/home-depot-will-pay-19-5-million-after-major-2014-n534881.

49. Trefis Team, 2015. *Home Depot: Will The Impact Of The Data Breach Be Significant?* 3 30. Accessed 8 28, 2017. https://www.forbes.com/sites/greatspeculations/2015/03/30/home-depot-will-the-impact-of-the-data-breach-be-significant/#2a5291204bf1.

50. Pierson, Brendan. 2017. *Anthem to pay record $115 million to settle U.S. lawsuits over data breach.* 6 23. Accessed 8 29, 2017. https://www.reuters.com/article/us-anthem-cyber-settlement-idUSKBN19E2ML.

51. Wikipedia. 2017. *HITRUST.* 7 1. Accessed 8 28, 2017. https://en.wikipedia.org/wiki/HITRUST.

52. Hackett, Robert. 2015. *Wired Jeep hack: Don't let stunt storytelling eclipse the message.* 7 22. Accessed 8 29, 2017. http://fortune.com/2015/07/22/wired-jeep-hack-takeaway/.

53. Drozhzhin, Alex. 2015. *Black Hat USA 2015: The full story of how that Jeep was hacked.* 8 6. Accessed 8 28, 2017. https://blog.kaspersky.com/blackhat-jeep-cherokee-hack-explained/9493/.

54. Newcomb, Alyssa. 2016. *'Jeep Hackers' Are Back With a Scary New Trick.* 8 5. Accessed 8 29, 2017. http://www.nbcnews.com/tech/tech-news/jeep-hackers-are-back-scary-new-trick-n623756.

55. Greenberg, Andy. 2015. *Chrysler and Harman Hit With a Class Action Complaint After Jeep Hack.* 8 4. Accessed 8 29, 2017. https://www.wired.com/2015/08/chrysler-harman-hit-class-action-complaint-jeep-hack/.

56. Wikipedia. 2017. *2011 PlayStation Network outage.* 8 23. Accessed 8 29, 2017. https://en.wikipedia.org/wiki/2011_PlayStation_Network_outage.

57. Williams, Martyn. 2011. *PlayStation Network hack will cost Sony $170M.* 5 23. Accessed 8 29, 2017. http://www.computerworld.com/article/2508315/computer-hardware/playstation-network-hack-will-cost-sony—170m.html.

58. Shino, Yuya. 2015. *Hack will cost Sony upwards of $35 million.* 2 4. Accessed 8 29, 2017. https://www.rt.com/usa/229291-sony-hack-cost-millions/.

59. Richwine, Lisa. 2014. *Cyber attack could cost Sony studio as much as $100 million.* 12 9. Accessed 8 29, 2017. http://www.reuters.com/article/us-sony-cybersecurity-costs-idUSKBN0JN2L020141209.

60. Greenberg, Adam. 2014. *Code Spaces shuts down following DDoS extortion, deletion of sensitive data*. 6 19. Accessed 8 28, 2017. https://www.scmagazine.com/code-spaces-shuts-down-following-ddos-extortion-deletion-of-sensitive-data/article/538612/.

61. Mimoso, Michael. 2014. *HACKER PUTS HOSTING SERVICE CODE SPACES OUT OF BUSINESS*. 6 18. Accessed 8 28, 2017. https://threatpost.com/hacker-puts-hosting-service-code-spaces-out-of-business/106761/.

62. Chappell, Bill. 2017. *'Petya' Ransomware Hits At Least 65 Countries; Microsoft Traces It To Tax Software*. 6 28. Accessed 8 29, 2017. http://www.npr.org/sections/thetwo-way/2017/06/28/534679950/petya-ransomware-hits-at-least-65-countries-microsoft-traces-it-to-tax-software.

63. Radware Ltd. 2017. *"BrickerBot" Results In PDoS Attack*. 4 5. Accessed 8 29, 2017. https://security.radware.com/ddos-threats-attacks/brickerbot-pdos-permanent-denial-of-service/.

64. Japan for Sustainability. 2011. *Japan's Power Shortages and Countermeasures After the Tohoku Earthquake, Tsunami and Fukushima Nuclear Crisis*. 4. Accessed 8 29, 2017. http://www.japanfs.org/en/news/archives/news_id030904.html.

65. RSA FraudAction Research Labs. 2011. *Anatomy of an Attack*. 4 1. Accessed 8 29, 2017. https://blogs.rsa.com/anatomy-of-an-attack/.

66. Wikipedia. 2017. *Defense in depth (computing)*. 7 5. Accessed 8 29, 2017. https://en.wikipedia.org/wiki/Defense_in_depth_(computing) .

67. Buntrock, Tim. 2017. *Protect your File Server against Ransomware by using FSRM and Powershell*. 2 13. Accessed 8 29, 2017. https://gallery.technet.microsoft.com/scriptcenter/Protect-your-File-Server-f3722fce.

68. Dunphy, John. 2004. *Protection Through Isolation*. 8 1. Accessed 8 29, 2017. https://mcpmag.com/articles/2004/08/01/protection-through-isolation.aspx.

69. Perlroth, Nicole. 2016. *Hackers Used New Weapons to Disrupt Major Websites Across U.S.* 10 21. Accessed 8 29, 2017. https://www.nytimes.com/2016/10/22/business/internet-problems-attack.html.

70. Woolf, Nicky, 2016. *DDoS attack that disrupted internet was largest of its kind in history, experts say*. 10 26. Accessed 8 29, 2017. https://www.theguardian.com/technology/2016/oct/26/ddos-attack-dyn-mirai-botnet.

71. Ragan, Steve. 2016. *Here are the 61 passwords that powered the Mirai IoT botnet*. 10 3. Accessed 8 29, 2017. http://www.csoonline.com/article/3126924/security/here-are-the-61-passwords-that-powered-the-mirai-iot-botnet.html.

72. Wright, Joshua. 2017. *Dispelling Common Bluetooth Misconceptions*. Accessed 8 29, 2017. https://www.sans.edu/cyber-research/security-laboratory/article/bluetooth.

73. Palmer, Danny. 2017. *How IoT hackers turned a university's network against itself*. 2 10. Accessed 8 29, 2017. http://www.zdnet.com/article/how-iot-hackers-turned-a-universitys-network-against-itself/.

74. Davis, Jeremy Seth. 2016. *Nest, other IoT devices, sent user info in the clear*. 10 21. Accessed 8 29, 2017. https://www.scmagazine.com/nest-other-iot-devices-sent-user-info-in-the-clear/article/529251/.

75. Schiffer, Alex. 2017. *How a fish tank helped hack a casino.* 7 21. Accessed 8 29, 2017. https://www.washingtonpost.com/news/innovations/wp/2017/07/21/how-a-fish-tank-helped-hack-a-casino/?utm_term=.807cbe305e5e.

76. Mark R. Warner. 2017. *Senators Introduce Bipartisan Legislation to Improve Cybersecurity of "Internet-of-Things" (IoT) Devices.* 8 1. Accessed 8 29, 2017. https://www.warner.senate.gov/public/index.cfm/pressreleases?id=06A5E941-FBC3-4A63-B9B4-523E18DADB36.

77. Knibbs, Kate, 2016. *Nest Thermostats Are Having Battery Problems and There's No Fix Yet.* 1 8. Accessed 8 29, 2017. http://gizmodo.com/nest-thermostats-are-having-battery-problems-and-theres-1751800309.

78. Industrial Internet Consortium. 2017. Accessed 8 29, 2017. http://www.iiconsortium.org/.

79. Martin, Chase. 2016. *U.S. Issues Guidelines For IoT Security.* 11 18. Accessed 8 29, 2017. https://www.mediapost.com/publications/article/289288/us-issues-guidelines-for-iot-security.html.

80. U.S. Department of Homeland Security. 2016. *STRATEGIC PRINCIPLES FOR SECURING THE INTERNET OF THINGS (IoT).* 11 15. Accessed 8 29, 2017. https://www.dhs.gov/sites/default/files/publications/Strategic_Principles_for_Securing_the_Internet_of_Things-2016-1115-FINAL....pdf.

81. Zurier, Steve. 2016. *Z-Wave Alliance Ups IoT security.* 12 12. Accessed 8 29, 2017. https://www.scmagazine.com/z-wave-alliance-ups-iot-security/article/578656/.

82. Z-Wave Alliance. 2016. *Territories.* Accessed 8 29, 2017. http://products.z-wavealliance.org/.

83. Cranor, Lorrie. 2016. *Time to rethink mandatory password changes.* 3 2. Accessed 8 29, 2017. https://www.ftc.gov/news-events/blogs/techftc/2016/03/time-rethink-mandatory-password-changes.

84. Zhang, Yinqian, Monrose, Fabian, and Reiter, Michael. 2010. *The Security of Modern Password Expiration: An Algorithmic Framework and Empirical Analysis.* Accessed 8 29, 2017. https://www.cs.unc.edu/~reiter/papers/2010/CCS.pdf.

85. Schneier, Bruce. 2016. *NIST is No Longer Recommending Two-Factor Authentication Using SMS.* 8 3. Accessed 8 29, 2017. https://www.schneier.com/blog/archives/2016/08/nist_is_no_long.html.

86. Pauli, Darren. 2016. *Standards body warned SMS 2FA is insecure and nobody listened.* 12 6. Accessed 8 29, 2017. https://www.theregister.co.uk/2016/12/06/2fa_missed_warning/.

87. Wikipedia. 2017. *Opportunistic encryption.* 7 17. Accessed 8 29, 2017. https://en.wikipedia.org/wiki/Opportunistic_encryption.

88. Wikipedia. 2017. *Opportunistic TLS.* 8 10. Accessed 8 29, 2017. https://en.wikipedia.org/wiki/Opportunistic_TLS.

89. Bossak, Kerry. 2017. *Yes, Ransomware can delete your Veeam backups.* 3 6. Accessed 8 29, 2017. https://forums.veeam.com/veeam-backup-replication-f2/yes-ransomware-can-delete-your-veeam-backups-t41500.html.

90. Microsoft Technet. 2015. *What is Active Directory Red Forest Design?* Accessed 8 29, 2017. https://social.technet.microsoft.com/wiki/contents/articles/37509. what-is-active-directory-red-forest-design.aspx.

91. Ultimate Windows Security. 2017. *Understanding "Red Forest": The 3-Tier Enhanced Security Admin Environment (ESAE) and Alternative Ways to Protect Privileged Credentials.* Accessed 8 29, 2017. https://www. ultimatewindowssecurity.com/webinars/register.aspx?id=1409.

92. Rouse, Margaret. 2014. *security information and event management (SIEM).* 12. Accessed 8 29, 2017. http://searchsecurity.techtarget.com/definition/security-information-and-event-management-SIEM.

93. PCI Security Standards Council LLC. 2016. *PCI DSS 3.2 Resource Guide.* https://www.pcisecuritystandards.org/pdfs/PCI_DSS_Resource_Guide_(003). pdf.

94. Wikipedia. *Model Audit Rule 205.* 4 4. Accessed 8 29, 2017. https://en.wikipedia. org/wiki/Model_Audit_Rule_205.

95. Wired. Accessed 8 29, 2017. https://www.wired.com/.

96. Krebs on Security. 2017. Accessed 8 29, 2017. http://krebsonsecurity.com/.

97. Schneier, Bruce. *Schneier on Security.* Accessed 8 29, 2017. https://www.schneier. com/.

98. Industrial Internet Consortium. 2017. Accessed 8 29, 2017. http://www. iiconsortium.org/.

99. BBC. 2017. *Hackers breached a dozen US nuclear plants, reports say.* 7 7. Accessed 8 29, 2017. http://www.bbc.com/news/world-us-canada-40538061.

100. Siegel, Robert and Perlroth, Nicole. 2017. *Shadow Brokers Group Leaks Stolen National Security Agency Hacking Tools.* 6 29. Accessed 8 29, 2017. http://www. npr.org/2017/06/29/534916031/shadow-brokers-group-leaks-stolen-national-security-agency-hacking-tools.

101. Moon, Mariella. 2017. *Ashley Madison will pay $11.2 million to data breach victims.* 7 16. Accessed 8 29, 2017. https://www.engadget.com/2017/07/16/ ashley-madison-lawsuit-settlement/.

102. Zetter, Kim. 2015. *Hackers Finally Post Stolen Ashley Madison Data.* 8 18. Accessed 8 29, 2017. https://www.wired.com/2015/08/happened-hackers-posted-stolen-ashley-madison-data/.

103. Barrett, Brian. 2017. *THAT ORANGE IS THE NEW BLACK LEAK WAS NEVER GOING TO PAY OFF.* 5 1. Accessed 8 29, 2017. https://www.wired. com/2017/05/orange-is-the-new-black-leak/.

104. McAtee, Carolyn. 2017. McAtee, Carolyn. 2017. *Hackers, beware! Girl Scouts to offer cybersecurity badges.* 6 21. Accessed 8 29, 2017. https://www.usatoday. com/story/tech/nation-now/2017/06/22/girl-scouts-offer-cybersecurity-badges/418443001/.

105. Bing, Chris. 2017. *Looking for an edge, cybersecurity firms spend big on quantum computing.* 2 2. Accessed 8 29, 2017. https://www.cyberscoop.com/looking-edge-cybersecurity-firms-spend-big-quantum-computing/.

106. FICO. 2017. *FICO® Enterprise Security Score*. Accessed 8 29, 2017. http://www.fico.com/en/products/fico-enterprise-security-score#overview.

107. Rouse, Margaret. 2017. *Software-defined networking (SDN)*. Accessed 8 29, 2017. http://searchsdn.techtarget.com/definition/software-defined-networking-SDN.

108. Sanghoee, Sanjay. 2015. *What Apple Is Missing About Cyber Security*. 4 17. Accessed 8 28, 2017. http://www.huffingtonpost.com/sanjay-sanghoee/what-apple-is-missing-abo_b_6689470.html.

109. Mansharamani, Vikram. 2016. *Why Apple vs. FBI might be the worst cybersecurity dilemma ever*. 3 11. Accessed 8 28, 2017. http://www.pbs.org/newshour/making-sense/why-apple-vs-fbi-might-be-the-worst-cybersecurity-dilemma-ever/.

110. Weintraub, Seth. 2016. *Apple File System (APFS) announced for 2017, scales 'from Apple Watch to Mac Pro' and focuses on encryption*. 6 13. Accessed 8 28, 2017. https://9to5mac.com/2016/06/13/apple-file-system-apfs/.

111. Steingold Volvo. 2014. *Volvo Commercial: "The Future of Safety"*. 10 28. Accessed 8 28 2017. https://www.youtube.com/watch?v=mmzPeoEDnc8.

112. Volvotips. 2012. *Volvo - safety is a beautiful thing (tv commercial)*. 10 1. Accessed 8 28, 2017. https://www.youtube.com/watch?v=dxyo2dOW6lA.

113. ZigWheels. 2009. *Volvo Safety Timeline*. 4 28. Accessed 8 28, 2017. https://www.youtube.com/watch?v=KtSOYEr-rYQ.

114. Wikipedia. 2017. *File Transfer Protocol*. 8 24. Accessed 8 29, 2017. https://en.wikipedia.org/wiki/File_Transfer_Protocol.

115. NIST. 2016. *Cybersecurity Framework FAQS Framework Basics*. 8 25. Accessed 8 28, 2017. https://www.nist.gov/cyberframework/cybersecurity-framework-faqs-framework-basics.

116. HITRUST Alliance. 2017. Accessed 8 28, 2017. https://hitrustalliance.net/.